Hazard Unlimited

By the same author

Slay Me Suddenly

Dangerfoot

Great Ideas in Communications

David and the Donkey

Red for Remembrance: The British Legion 1921–1971

Hazard Unlimited

THE STORY OF LLOYD'S OF LONDON

ANTONY BROWN

PETER DAVIES : LONDON

Peter Davies Ltd
15 Queen St, Mayfair, London, W1X 8BE
LONDON MELBOURNE TORONTO
JOHANNESBURG AUCKLAND

First published 1973
432 01905 7

Printed in Great Britain by
Morrison and Gibb, London and Edinburgh

Contents

Illustrations

Between pages 50 *and* 51

Between pages 146 *and* 147

Preface

THIS book is different in several ways from others that have been written about Lloyd's. My first aim has been to show the ordinary reader how the market works and to capture something of its atmosphere and special flavour.

Second, Lloyd's influence is today world-wide. I have tried to show how something that began as a purely marine market has now become the world's greatest centre for insuring anything from an oil refinery to a fleet of jumbo jets.

Most previous books about Lloyd's have been written as straightforward history. Because this ground is relatively well-worn, I have consciously avoided it. I have told the story of the coffee house comparatively briefly in Chapter Two. Thereafter I have gone back into history where it seemed relevant, or where, as in the story of Lloyd's part in the invention of the life-boat, I have been able to bring forward new facts. But on the whole this book is intended to complement the standard history by D. E. W. Gibb,* rather than to replace it. At the same time I must acknowledge the great debt which any writer on Lloyd's must owe to Gibb, and I am indebted to the Committee of Lloyd's for permission to quote from it.

Any book of this kind is in a real sense a collaboration between author and subject. The pleasantest part of my task is to thank the very many people at Lloyd's who have helped me. I am indebted to everyone mentioned in these pages for their courtesy and kindness, but I must especially thank Mr Paul Dixey, the Chairman of Lloyd's, for his kindness in reading the

* GIBB, D. E. W.: *Lloyd's of London. A Study in Individualism* (Macmillan, London, 1957).

manuscript at various stages and for his constant help and encouragement. Mr Henry Chester has been an invaluable guide and adviser on many aspects of the market apart from those pages in which he figures. I should also like to thank Mr Peter Wright of Sedgwick Forbes for his guidance on the brokers' chapter. Mr Roy Merrett found time in an active retirement to help and advise me on the Indonesian story. I owe a special debt to the Hon. Mrs Liliana Archibald for preparing the index. Of the many underwriters who have helped me I must especially thank Mr Frank Barber and Mr R. C. J. Gordon.

Among the Corporation staff I am particularly grateful to Mr Dick Rutherford for his patience in explaining the world of claims, and for letting me have access to his files on Suez.

Mr Douglas Greenall and Mr Len Kirby of Lloyd's Information Department have been untiringly helpful in suggesting material and in reading the manuscript at all stages, though I must stress that all opinions expressed in the book are my own. I would also like to thank Mr Paul Dalton for the use of the photograph of London Bridge. Mr Keith Brown, Lloyd's American attorney, and Mr John Smith of Chicago, have both been indispensable guides to the American side of Lloyd's business.

Among people outside Lloyd's I must thank Mr Howard of the Salvage Association, and Mr Harry Thurston. I am also most grateful to Mr Lodder and the directors of the Verolme Dock and Shipbuilding Company for their courtesy and hospitality in Rotterdam. I am much indebted to Mrs Heather Ging of Tyne-Tees Television and Miss Orde of South Shields Public Library for their help on the story of Henry Greathead; and to my secretary, Diana Cookson, for her patience and helpfulness.

Finally I must thank David Larner of Lloyd's Information Office whose assistance, encouragement and enthusiasm have far exceeded anything called for in the line of duty. I am also most grateful for his help and Mr R. H. Brown's help in compiling a glossary, for the benefit of those who do not (as I did not before I began my researches) know a marine name from a deductible or a wet risk.

It is for such readers, above all, that this book has been written.

PART ONE

The Tradition

I

The Room

If you walk from Bank Station towards Leadenhall Street, you will find yourself in one of the City's small worlds. As other parts of the City exist for furs or fish, Leadenhall Street exists for ships. It may be anything from Cunard to the Greek Hull Pool, from P & O to Hispania Marine. In the small streets around St Mary Axe there are so many offices of shipbrokers, ship-insurers and ship-owners that you almost expect the streets themselves to have water in them, like Amsterdam or Venice.

There is Africa House and there was once East India House, and towering above them all, itself a bit like a landlocked liner, is Lloyd's. It has no sign over it and it needs none, for it is less of an office than an institution—the home of the most historic insurance market in the world.

But what really is Lloyd's? Everyone has heard of it, yet few could tell you much about it, except perhaps that it insures ships. The reality is both broader and deeper. This very English institution is global in its interests and outlook. It is also very traditional, yet a key part of the tradition has always been to innovate and pioneer.

In the history of business enterprise there is nothing quite like Lloyd's of London. For the last two hundred years of its history, its heart and centre has been a room called simply *the* Room. Let us begin by seeing what happens in it.

Originally the Room was part of a coffee house in seventeenth-century London. Today it is roughly the size of the Concorde's hangar, air-conditioned, sound-proofed and equipped with every modern aid. Yet in essence it has not changed. If you go into the Room today you will still see what happened at Lloyd's in the seventeenth century.

You will see underwriters sitting talking to brokers, much as their counterparts did in the coffee house. You will see a man in a red robe, known as the Caller, who intones the names of brokers. His counterpart in the coffee house recited the names of overdue ships, but the principle is the same. There are other men in blue uniforms, who in an ordinary business house would be called porters, commissionaires and messengers. At Lloyd's, because of its origins, they are still called waiters.

As you begin to take in the geography of the Room you will see that it has one main feature—the rows of underwriters' boxes. These, too, stem from the coffee house—in essence a box consists of two wooden pews with a table between them. Anything from six to a dozen people can sit in a box, and if you look down on the Room from the gallery you get the impression of hundreds of separate groups, packed in their boxes like commuters in a crowded train.

Why, you might ask, should Lloyd's cling to this archaic custom? The point is that now, as in the 1760s, Lloyd's is not an insurance office but a market—the only place in the world where you can find so many potential insurers under one roof. The underwriter's box is really his pitch in the market—if a broker cannot place his risk at one box, he moves to another.

If, as often happens, the risk is too big for a single insurer, then the broker will find plenty of others in the Room to take a share of it. Thus he can complete the whole insurance, even on the most complex or large-scale risk, within a single market.

But before we go into the procedure in detail, let us look at the people who, over three hundred years, have made Lloyd's unique: the underwriters.

Once in the 1890s a famous Lloyd's man was asked by a lady visitor to explain the market. He made a celebrated answer.

'Individually, madam,' he said, 'we are underwriters. Collectively, we are Lloyd's.' Over nearly a century the definition has not been bettered—the point is that people work *at* Lloyd's, not for it. The underwriters are answerable for certain things to the Committee of Lloyd's, but not for their underwriting. The Committee is there to see that the market is properly run, and that its reputation for integrity is maintained. Beyond that, the underwriter is his own man.

Perhaps it is because of the very looseness of the organization that Lloyd's has always evoked a special kind of loyalty. There is a sense of belonging which would be hardly imaginable in a conventional business. Nobody ever thinks of leaving Lloyd's; most members will tell you, without embarrassment, that they love the place.

One famous Lloyd's man described to me how, as a young clerk, he used to dream of the day he might become an underwriter. All underwriters have their own special flourish when putting their initials to a risk; and he had spent hours optimistically practising his own initial. I asked him to show me how it looked, and he wrote it lovingly, like an artist, on a page of my pad. 'I don't know how many times I've written it since then,' he said, 'but I've never lost the sense of magic.'

'Personal friendship and the great liberality I have always found induces me to do my business with them,' said a broker of the underwriters in 1810, and the feeling is still there. One former Lloyd's broker told me a story that had happened years ago, over an August bank holiday. On the Friday before the holiday one of his clients posted him an order for insurance on a cargo of fish that was going to South America. The ship sailed over the weekend and by the time the market opened on Tuesday morning she had gone aground on some rocks off the coast of Portugal.

'In those days,' said the broker, 'there was no such thing as automatic cover, and of course the order for the insurance didn't arrive till the Tuesday morning.' He went to the Room, and sought out the underwriter with whom he would normally have placed the risk. It happened to be Neville Dixey,* who later became Chairman of Lloyd's. 'He looked me in the eye and asked was this a risk I would normally have brought to him first? I said it was, and he picked up his pen and wrote it—the insurance on a cargo that he knew was already floating out to the Atlantic.'

Once in the eighteenth century the existence of Lloyd's was threatened by the spread of a kind of underwriting which was virtually gambling. A group of Lloyd's men removed themselves from the scene, took the best of the tradition with them and set up the coffee house elsewhere. Again, in the early part of this century when safeguards were less strict than today, Lloyd's integrity was threatened by a defaulting underwriter. Rather than let its good name go down, every man in the market paid a share of what was owing—it amounted to nearly a quarter of a million pounds. In both cases, it could be argued, Lloyd's men were acting in what was ultimately their own interest. But there was also something else—the feeling that the special quality of the place must be preserved at all costs.

Till recently, Lloyd's had the reputation of being a kind of gentlemen's club, but that is true no longer. There are still those who come to Lloyd's because their fathers did, but many more who have come up from being clerks in the Room. I met one underwriter who was descended from the poet Coleridge, and another who was the son of a gas-fitter from Hackney. If there is an élite in the market, it is not social but professional. The boxes you see most crowded with brokers are those of what are known as leading underwriters; there are leading underwriters at Lloyd's whose progress through the Room has something of the verve and dignity of a Renaissance duke.

To be 'leading' in this sense does not mean merely to be prominent. Literally, the leading underwriter 'leads' a risk. This means that he is the first person to whom the broker

* Also, incidentally, the father of the present Chairman.

shows it. With the broker, he will work out the rate for the risk, or even decide it is unacceptable as offered. Though he does not bind the market, he sets a rate for the business. Following underwriters will write their line, or proportion of the risk, at the same rate because they trust his judgement.

The leading underwriter may guide the market but every underwriter is perpetually making decisions. Every moment he is on his box he is assessing a risk. Each time he accepts one, he is backing his decision with his own money. 'They've got to be tougher than nails,' said one visiting American broker. 'There's nobody like a Lloyd's underwriter. It's the lonesomest occupation I know—there's nowhere else where you sit all day at the buckstop.' Perhaps for this reason, modesty is the least apparent virtue in the Room. The underwriters make up the most aggressively intelligent insurance market in the world, and know it.

Because of its intense individualism there is none of the rigid orthodoxy that you find in most City institutions—at Lloyd's, you feel, they like to be a little unpredictable. Recently the members elected as chairman an underwriter whose political views were known to be radical: it was the kind of mildly unconventional touch that Lloyd's men rather like. One member of Lloyd's owns race-horses. A lot, particularly marine underwriters, have boats. 'You wouldn't think messing about in a fourteen-foot dinghy could help you to insure an oil tanker,' said one, 'but it's surprising what you can learn about wind and weather.'

In a way such details are a pointer to Lloyd's style—if the underwriters have a professional credo, it would be a mixture of accumulated expertise, flair and the acquisition of odd bits of useful knowledge.

Often they have a touch of temperament unusual in the City; along with the style and charm there is an edge of gritty toughness, and because of the immaculacy of the charm it is not always easy to discern which characteristic is overlaying which.

At one box I listened while a broker tried to convince the underwriter that a particular client of his was a reformed character. This ship-owner, he said, had come to London and had lunch at the broker's office, and explained how he had spent the whole winter re-equipping his fleet.

Despite the broker's pleading, the underwriter had got his head down. 'He may have had lunch with you,' he said. 'He's still a crook.'

The broker laughed, as if the underwriter must be allowed his joke, but after another twenty minutes they were still talking. Later I asked the underwriter what would happen about the risk and he said he did a lot of business with that particular broking firm, and you had to keep a good relationship going. 'It's not the sort of thing you can have spoilt by a difficult client,' he said. 'In the end I'll probably write it.'

It would mean something to a Lloyd's man if you told him that a non-marine name had written a wet risk: like all highly individual atmospheres, the Room has its own jargon. You can get to know a good deal about the market without ever learning the difference between a deductible and excess-of-loss. What you do need to know is that the underwriter never signs a policy, he writes it—as other people might write books or sonnets, Lloyd's underwriters write jet airliners and nuclear power-stations. The piece of paper the broker shows him is called a Slip. If he accepts the risk on the Slip he writes what is called his Line, or proportion of the insurance. When he does this he is accepting the risk for his Syndicate which is composed of what are known as Names—or what other businesses would call his sleeping partners.

Apart from direct risks, the slip the broker offers may be for Reinsurance. It may sound paradoxical, but an underwriter, having taken on a risk, will often seek to unload some of his liability. To do this he reinsures with another syndicate—thus making certain that if there is a loss it will not be more than his syndicate can bear. Often the client in such a case will be an outside insurance company—Lloyd's, as the largest market of this kind in the world, reinsures not only British companies but most of the leading American ones.

All this, like much else in the Room, we shall come back to. Meanwhile there is something else which is at the heart of the tradition—an almost restlessly inventive urge to pioneer. It was a Lloyd's underwriter who wrote the first burglary risk in the early part of this century. Today the risk is more likely to be on pollution in California or a new kind of drilling-rig in the Arctic, but Lloyd's response is the same—to try to work out a way of insuring something that the rest of the insurance world is still alarmed by. 'Of course it's a profitable business,' said one underwriter, 'and I wouldn't be in it if I wasn't making money. But I wouldn't be in it either if it wasn't fun.'

Another underwriter said that the whole point was that at Lloyd's there was no such thing as a fixed rate: if you went to an ordinary insurance company they would look it up in a book, but at Lloyd's every rate and every risk was different. Some time before, he said, a broker had come and asked him if he would write a risk on a railroad in America, and his deputy on the box had said they didn't write railroads. 'I said the hell with it, the rules are there to be broken. So we started writing railroads, and we've made a healthy profit.'

If there were such a thing as a typical Lloyd's man, he might be a bit like Mr Geoffrey Eliot. Mr Eliot is fifty-seven, a leading underwriter in the aviation market who has pioneered every kind of risk from hovercraft to jumbo jets. Like a lot of Lloyd's men, he looks as if he would be more at home in the open air. Tall, greying and slightly stooping, he is an immensely popular figure in the market—but also, you feel, the kind of man who respects standards and expects others to respect them. He would never have lunch with a broker, he told me, in case the broker might think it was a way of getting favours. On his box he is known as the Master, and you feel it is a joke not untinged with respect.

I asked Mr Eliot what good underwriting implied, and he said that a good underwriter was the one who could say no nicely enough for the brokers to come back next day. The most difficult thing was the speed at which you had to make decisions —it was why, he added with a twinkle, underwriters were difficult at home. 'You get home and your wife says do you want pudding tonight and you rap out yes. It's because of being on the box all day, having to decide things quickly.'

The afternoon I sat on Mr Eliot's box there were five other people: his deputy, Mr Robin Bell, Mr Eliot's son Robin who is learning to be an underwriter, and three other underwriting staff. Mr Eliot himself was very much the man in command, and treated all brokers with courteous, patrician humour. Favoured brokers at the Eliot box, or even difficult ones, will get offered a sweet from a tin of Parkinson's Old Fashioned Humbugs. The box gets through an 8-lb jar of them a fortnight.

Otherwise the accoutrements of the box are few—with six people crammed into an area eight feet by four, Mr Eliot explained, there wasn't much room for extras. On a kind of superstructure built on the desk there were a lot of fat metal files, an atlas or so, and a well-thumbed copy of *Jane's All the World's Aircraft*. Otherwise there seemed to be a great deal of pink blotting-paper, sheets of which are delivered at each box daily by the waiters. Even in the age of the biro pen no underwriter would think of writing a risk with anything but a fountain pen—there are even a couple of syndicates where they write with quills.

When I arrived at the box Mr Eliot was talking to a broker. Most tend to be young, but this was an older man who carefully addressed all the underwriters as 'sir'. What was being discussed was not a new insurance but a completed one—it was for a very large risk on one of the Far Eastern airlines. As a leading underwriter in the aviation market Mr Eliot had been the first to write a line on the slip. Since then it had been oversubscribed or, as Lloyd's calls it, overdone: a broker will sometimes get more support than he needs on a risk, simply because in the early stages he will have encouraged underwriters to write him a large line. The broker wanted to know if Mr Eliot would mind reducing his line.

'That'll sign down.' Mr Eliot nodded and passed the slip to his deputy. The original line had been for 3½ per cent of thirty million dollars—now, he said, it would be reduced to 1·4. The deputy wrote the details in one of the fat ledgers and made a note about reinsurance. On a risk of this scale, he explained, the underwriter may reinsure to spread the load. The skill of this lay in reinsuring enough but not too much, so it didn't eat up your profits.

While the deputy was making his notes Robin Eliot asked me to pass a bottle of ink from the drawer in front of me: in the restricted space there was a feeling of having a picnic in a crowded beach hut. Next to the bottle of ink in the drawer was what looked like a book of matches—in fact it contained a miniature set of darts. Robin saw me looking at it, grinned and produced from his own drawer a tiny cricket set, complete with bat and wicket. 'That's what we do when things are quiet,' he said. 'Sometimes we've had half a dozen brokers out there fielding.'

The next broker was youthful and long-haired—he looked as if he would have liked to ask the underwriter to move up and let him sit on the bench, but didn't quite like to with Mr Eliot. The slip was for a fleet of helicopters working in the timber trade in Alaska, and Mr Eliot didn't seem too keen. Ten million dollars was a lot of money, he said, with grave courtesy, and he didn't like the look of the premium; Robin whispered to me that these things could produce horrendous claims. One of them had crashed last year, and killed six people.

'I don't think I want to be in this business at all,' said Mr Eliot, politely. 'I only hope you can finish it.' The broker looked hurt, accepted an old-fashioned humbug, and went off. Meanwhile another broker had come up, and Mr Eliot asked the deputy how he was getting on with the reinsurance. 'You see how much you can do,' he said amiably, 'while I deal with the next rogue.'

This time the risk seemed a somewhat unlikely one—an American insurance company wanted some re-insurance on any claims that might arise from having to search for missing oil rigs in the Greater Boston area. The company didn't plan to use their own aircraft but to hire one with a pilot, which was apparently called a wet lease.

'You say they go out looking for missing oil rigs?' Mr Eliot looked a bit unbelieving. 'It's not a very easy thing to lose, is it, an oil rig?'

The broker said he supposed it must happen, or they wouldn't be wanting the insurance.

'All the same. I can't rate you a passenger-carrying aircraft without knowing what kind of aircraft.'

'I realize that.' The broker began to look as if even he thought the whole thing was a bit unlikely, but meanwhile Mr Eliot had started doing sums on a bit of paper.

'It boils down to the fact that they want a million dollars BI/PD?'

Robin Eliot explained to me that this meant Bodily Injury and Property Damage. Meanwhile the broker had begun to look hopeful. Since Mr Eliot had already said it wasn't very easy to lose an oil rig, he supposed there wouldn't be much of a premium.

Mr Eliot drew himself up slightly. 'It wouldn't be less than $500.'

'I think it's out of the question.' The broker shook his head, and Mr Eliot studied him with the air of a tolerant man dealing with a delinquent. 'Say 300?'

'400 and finish.' Mr Eliot picked up his pen, which is the moment they say the broker should stop talking. The broker did so. Mr Eliot wrote a graceful initial on the slip, then stamped it.

By now it was half-past four, and the stream of brokers had begun to recede. I said goodbye to Mr Eliot, strolled back past the Casualty Board where the clerks were noting down the details of fires, shipwrecks, all the imaginable and unimaginable disasters against which Lloyd's insures the world. Soon the great Room would be empty as a silent theatre. There would be nothing but crumpled pink blotting paper in the aisles and the ghosts, if underwriters have ghosts, straying from the shadows.

It seemed a moment to pause, and look back to the beginning.

2

The Coffee House

To think of a coffee house as a place of business requires a certain effort of the imagination. One can imagine a folk-opera being written within range of a modern Gaggia machine, but hardly the insurance of a ship's hull. Yet in seventeenth-century London the coffee house was something between a specific market place and a club. The regular customer would have a comfortable chair by the fire. He would be waited on, most likely, by a pretty waitress. Not only was the actual Coffee or Kauphy, as it was known, non-intoxicating; it was, according to the advertisements, positively life-giving. 'It is excellent', ran the advertisement for Pasqua Rosee's coffee house in St Michael's Alley, off Cornhill, 'to prevent and cure the dropsy, gout and scurvy. It is known by experience to be better than any other drying drink for people in years, or children that have any running humours upon them, as the king's evil, etc. It is a most excellent remedy against the spleen, hypochondriac winds, and the like. It will prevent drowsiness, and make one fit for business.'

The contemporary copywriter's use of words in the last phrase was particularly well aimed—above all, the coffee house was the place where a man would conduct his business. Of London's 300 coffee houses in the reign of Charles II, most catered for a specific group. For the poets and wits of Covent Garden, there was Button's, the Bedford, and Will's, where Dryden had his own chair. The doctors would go to Child's in St Paul's Churchyard, close to the Royal College of Surgeons. For the lawyers there were the coffee houses on the south side of Fleet Street; the scholars and journalists went to the Grecian on the north side. Nearer Temple Bar was the evidently notorious Rainbow, whose proprietor was charged, in 1657, with 'making and selling a sort of liquor called Kauffee, being a great nuisance and prejudice to the neighbourhood'.

For the merchants and bill brokers in the city there was Hain's in Birchin Lane, or Garraway's where they sold ships by the old method of candle-auctions. Bidding would go on while the candle burnt down an inch. A pin would be stuck in the bottom of it and the last bid had to be made before the pin dropped out as the surrounding candle melted. It must have been a dramatic sight, the faces of the bidders lit by candlelight in the silence during which – as the phrase has come down to us – you could hear a pin drop.

Sometimes – and in these days before Lloyd's it seems likely to have happened most often at Garraway's – a merchant in some other line of business would set up a small sideline of insuring ships. In the nature of things there were probably few of these insurers, or underwriters as they were historically known from the fact that they wrote their line and proportion of the risk under each other's. So we can imagine the underwriter sitting by the fire at Garraway's, or the broker with a risk to place hawking it from one coffee house to another, probably from Garraway's to Jonathan's, from Jonathan's to the Barbadoes coffee house in Change Alley.

But on the whole that is about all we can safely imagine. From those early days of underwriting, hardly a record has come down. Just occasionally we have the details of an actual deal. Truthful to his diary if nothing else, Samuel Pepys records how he once passed up the opportunity of making a dishonest penny:

> Up and to Alderman Backewell's where Sir W. Rider, by appointment, met us to consult about the insuring of our hempe ship from Archangell . . . Back to the Coffee-house, and then to the 'Change where Sir W. Rider and I did bid 15 per cent., and nobody will take it under 20 per cent., and the lowest was 15 per cent., premium,

and 15 more to be abated in case of losse, which we did not think fit without order to give . . . called at the Coffee-house, and there by great accident hear that a letter is coming that our ship is safe come to Newcastle. With this news I went like an asse, presently to Alderman Backewell and told him of it . . . Now what an opportunity had I to have concealed this and seemed to have made an insurance and got £100 with the least trouble and danger in the whole world. This troubles me to think I should be so oversoon.

The date of that diary entry is 23 November 1663. Three years later came the Great Fire, and an end to the physical geography of the city as Pepys and his contemporaries had known it.

Gradually, through the next two decades, the ruined areas began to be rebuilt. But the new houses round the Royal Exchange were of stone, and consequently commanded high rents. The result was that a new centre of commerce sprang up at the eastern end of the city—the part which lies roughly between Leadenhall Street and the Tower, and which had been largely untouched by the Fire of London. It was in this area, in Tower Street off Eastcheap, that Edward Lloyd began his coffee house somewhere in the 1680s.

Who was Edward Lloyd? And why did his coffee house come to be linked with marine insurance?

The answer to the second question is relatively easy—the coffee house was close to the Tower and what is now the Pool of London. Its location alone must have made it a natural meeting place for seamen, ship's captains and ship-owners.

Of Edward Lloyd himself we know almost nothing. He seems to have been born around 1648, to have been a church warden, and three times married. He was a member of the Framework Knitters' Company, membership of which may have come down to him through his father. When he died in 1713 he was buried in St Mary Woolnoth's in Lombard Street.

What we do know about Lloyd, though, is that his business seems to have prospered from the beginning. By 1688, at least, it must have been well known. For in that year we find the first written reference to Lloyd's, in an advertisement in the *London Gazette*.

The advertisement was inserted by one Edward Bransby of Derby, who had apparently been robbed of five watches and was offering a guinea reward to anyone who could give information about the theft.

Edward Bransby of Derby must have been an observant man, for he described the thief in detail—middle-sized, with black, curled hair and pockholes, not to mention a beaver hat and a brown riding-coat. Whether Bransby ever got his watches back we do not know. The point is that in his advertisement he asked for any information about the thief to be reported to Lloyd's. By 1688 the coffee house must have been at least well enough known to occur to a citizen of Derby as a place which anyone in London would be likely to find.

Three years later in 1691, we find Lloyd moving to much larger and presumably more expensive premises in Lombard Street. Here the coffee house was to remain for the next eighty years—years when the foundation of Lloyd's as a centre of marine insurance would be laid.

It is worth noting that at no stage was Lloyd himself concerned with the actual business of insuring ships. His role was simply to provide a coffee house. True, he must have become fairly knowledgeable about marine insurance, but only in the sense that one might expect the secretary of the Athenaeum to be well informed about bishops.

All the same, Edward Lloyd was clearly a man of reputation. In 1703, for instance, when Britain was at war and nobody could leave the country without a passport, his name comes up as a reference fifteen times in three months. Germans bound for the Hanseatic ports, Englishmen going to the West Indies, seem all to have asked Lloyd to vouch for their credentials.

There were less respectable trades as well. A newspaper of 2 January 1793 carried this advertisement:

A negro maid aged about sixteen years, named Bess, having on a stript stuff waistcoat and peticoat, is much peck't with the Small Pox, and hathe lost a piece of her left ear, speaks English well, ran away from her Master Captain Benjamin Quelch, on Tuesday, the 8th of December. A Guinea for anybody delivering her to Mr Edward Lloyd.

Such dabblings in the slave trade were probably taken for granted by the kind of people who frequented Edward Lloyd's. Meanwhile there were other and more admirable ways in which he seems to have gone beyond his role as the proprietor of a coffee house, and it was these, more than anything, which were the key to his success.

All coffee houses saw it as their duty to supply their customers with pens and ink, but Edward Lloyd went one further. He supplied them with news. He employed runners who would work from the coffee house down to the wharves, picking up the news of ship arrivals. When there were casualties which might be important to his customers, an announcement would be made to the coffee house at large by one of the waiters who was known as the Kidney. 'It is the custom at Lloyd's,' wrote Steele in the *Tatler*, 'upon the first coming in of the news, to order a youth, who officiates as the *Kidney* of the coffee house, to get into the pulpit, and read every paper with a loud and distinct voice, while the whole audience are sipping their respective liquors.'

By 1696, Lloyd's whole conception of a news and intelligence service had gone much further. By then if a ship-owner in the West Country wanted to sell a ship, he would send an inventory and description of her to Lloyd's, and put an advertisement in the daily papers telling prospective customers that further particulars might be had at the coffee house in Lombard Street.

From here the next step was clear. In 1696 Lloyd brought out his own newspaper of shipping movements. Under the title *Lloyd's News* it was, the imprint said, 'Printed for Edward Lloyd (Coffee man) in Lombard Street'.

Modest as the imprint sounds, Lloyd must by now have been in a booming way of business, with his coffee house the acknowledged centre for anyone concerned with ships. Somewhere, probably early on in the Lombard Street days, the chairs and tables had come to be replaced by boxes for the customers to sit at.

Soon the pulpit from which the Kidney addressed the customers was being used for auctions too. The candle sales, once famous at Garraway's, now took place at Lloyd's, and as early as 1692 there is a reference to a sale by candle at Lloyd's of three ships from as far away as 'Plimmouth'. There were sales of Turkey coffee, Alicant wines, and even horses.

By 1700 the sales had become an everyday feature of London life—so much so that the author of a contemporary doggerel called *The Wealthy Shopkeeper and Charitable Citizen* wrote of his hero that he went:

> 'Now to Lloyd's Coffee House: he never fails
> To read the letters and attend the Sales.'

By the turn of the century, in fact, we can begin to see the first shadowy outline of the modern Lloyd's. The coffee house had become a centre for everything which could be called maritime—shipping news, ship sales, ships' cargoes. Already the setting and the props were there, the pulpit and benches which were fore-runners of the boxes. So were the small-part players like the Kidney, later to become the Caller.

What was still missing was the central figure—the Lloyd's underwriter.

Long before 1700 people had been insuring ships. Probably the Greeks and Phoenicians had insured against maritime loss, but the first existing record comes from a Roman edict of AD 533, in the reign of the Emperor Justinian. It fixed the interest on all loans at 6 per cent but made an exception for the rate of marine insurance. This was allowed to go as high as 12 per cent

—the practice of usury being thus restrained, wrote Gibbon, 'except in this perilous adventure'.

Over the centuries various forms of marine insurance flicker and fade across the skyline of our knowledge. We learn that the Hanseatic merchants of northern Europe had an insurance centre based at Bruges. In 1432 the city of Barcelona laid down the first recorded statute for insuring ships. In those days when a vessel was lost, the circumstances of her loss were seldom known. If a ship had not been heard of for six months, said the statute of Barcelona, she would be regarded as lost, and the owner could claim from the insurer.

Meanwhile the first form of marine insurance in Britain had been started by a group of Hanseatic merchants who came to London in the fourteenth century. In those days Britain had hardly begun to be a trading nation. The Germans seem to have come as somewhat unwelcome colonists, and to have been treated as such by the Londoners. To protect them from attacks by the mob, they were allowed a piece of land on the site of what is now Cannon Street Station.

Here they proceeded to build a kind of fortification rather grimly known as the Steelyard. Within it they carried on every conceivable kind of business and lived a depressingly disciplined life. They ate communally, were not allowed to marry or even visit women, and the Steelyard door was firmly barred at night.

Few spectacles are less attractive than that of someone trying to make a lot of money when he has nothing agreeable to spend it on, and there is something a little unnerving about the thought of these celibate Germans immured behind their fortress in the Steelyard. All the same they have their place in history as London's first underwriters. Working along the lines laid down by the Hanseatic League, they carried on their business throughout the reign of Queen Elizabeth, but in their later years had the competition of another group of foreign immigrants. These were the Lombards, who had been expelled from Italy in the thirteenth century and had built up a flourishing business centre in London by the sixteenth. From them we get the name of Lombard Street and the word *polizza* – a promise – from which our word 'policy' derives. Writing of the site of the Royal Exchange, the London historian John Stow records that 'here anciently the Lombards or Bankers dwelt, and so they did to the days of Queen Elizabeth'.

The last words are significant. By Elizabeth's reign the merchants of London no longer needed to be taught their trade by the Lombards or the Germans. A recent chairman of Lloyd's observed that in the twentieth century an emergent country needed two symbols of its independence—a national airline and a national insurance company. In Elizabethan England there was something of the same spirit, and at the opening of the Queen's first Parliament in 1559 Sir Nicholas Bacon had asked: 'Is there any, think you, so mad that, having a range of houses in peril of fire, would not gladly pluck down part to have the rest preserved and saved? Doth not the wise merchant in every adventure of danger, give part to have the rest assured?'

Twelve years before Bacon's speech, the first surviving English marine policy had been issued. It was taken out by a man named John Broke, on a ship called the *Santa Maria*, bound with a cargo of wine from Cadiz to London. On Broke's policy there were only two underwriters, but as time went on the numbers grew. By 1555 we find as many as twenty-five underwriters putting their names to a risk.

Who were these underwriters of the Elizabethan age? Most were probably bankers and moneylenders writing insurance as a sideline. But a little later there occurs the name of the first professional insurance man in Britain: Richard Candeler, who in 1574 was granted a patent or monopoly of 'all manner of assewrances polleycies intimacions Renunciacions and other thinges whatsoever . . . upon any shippe or shippes goods or merchaundize'.

By the middle of the seventeenth century the number of underwriters was growing. In the Bodleian Library at Oxford there is a broker's account book containing thirty-one notes of risks and premiums written by underwriters scattered around the City from Mark Lane to Threadneedle Street and Crutched Friars. Over the next thirty years one can imagine them shifting their base of operations to Edward Lloyd's coffee house, first by the Tower and then in Lombard Street.

Yet in the years immediately following Lloyd's move to Lombard Street, our knowledge of the underwriters is still vague. Here and there we get a flash of insight. We learn that one Daniel Foe nearly ruined himself by writing marine insurance. (Later he was to put his nautical interest to better use by writing, in the other sense, *Robinson Crusoe*.)

Somewhere in the early 1700s we come across a dark story of a broker's fraud on a ship called the *Vansittart*. Unable, or perhaps not wanting, to complete his risk, the broker had invented two fictitious names of insurers and put them on the slip. The *Vansittart* went down, and the broker was found out.

The repercussions of this affair seem to have gone on long afterwards. As late as 1717 we find a group of office-keepers (as brokers were usually called at the time) defending themselves against the charge that such practices still happened:

> We do in answer to such foul false and malicious a charge declare that we detest all such vile actions and do challenge all the merchants in England to produce one instance of any policy made in either of our offices underwrote with a fictitious name . . . The policy hinted at on the *Vansittart* was made by a person since dead who was not an office-keeper but one who acted as a broker for discounting notes and did sometimes make policies.

Meanwhile, when names were written on an insurance slip, whose names were they? Was the marine underwriter's trade still a sort of sideline to some other business? Or had a new kind of figure appeared—an individual underwriter whose profession it was to write insurance, and especially insurance on ships?

All the evidence suggests that he had. And during the next

few years his struggle for survival was to be crucial in the making of Lloyd's.

Over the years that led up to 1720 a new element had been thrown into the situation. This was the demand for the setting up of new insurance companies under Royal Charter—an answer, so it was thought, to the frenzy of speculation that had gripped the City of London since the South Sea Bubble. Among the speculators there had been a vast proliferation of small companies seeking to cash in on insurance against everything from fires – presumably fashionable since 1666 – to highway robbery. You could get policies against death from gin-drinking, against being lied to by your business competitors, even a policy on what was delicately described as Female Chastity.

In effect the call for new chartered companies meant the end of these speculative insurers. Most probably they deserved to go down—but the trouble was that under the new plan, the individual underwriters seemed bound to go down with them. Given the prospect of large new companies operating under a Royal Charter, there seemed no chance of any individual underwriters surviving.

To the astonished delight of the underwriters, this was not how things turned out. In 1720 charters were granted to two new companies, the Royal Exchange and London Assurance. Both charters laid down that marine insurance could not be written by any other company or corporation.

But – and this is the point – there was no exclusion of individual underwriters. Ironically, they had been immensely helped by the very thing which had seemed bound to destroy them.

Why had this happened? Perhaps the potential power of the individual underwriters had been overlooked in the general concern to put a stop to the mushroom companies. Possibly those who had drafted the Act had been so certain of the new chartered companies' success that they had scarcely bothered about a few individuals who intended to write marine business. Almost by an accident of law, it seemed, the individual underwriter had been given his own charter too. From now on he could write marine business free from the competition of the small companies.

There was only one proviso—in the event of a loss, the whole of the underwriter's accumulated premiums were to be made available to satisfy the assured.

In terms of the future of Lloyd's, the guarantee would be prophetic.

Almost immediately it became clear that the competition from the two new chartered companies was going to be far less of a threat than the individual underwriters had feared. From the start both the London Assurance and the Royal Exchange found themselves in difficulties, largely due to their fishing in the troubled waters of the South Sea Bubble. Moreover neither of them seemed to be so skilled or even interested in marine insurance as they were in fire business. Soon the individual underwriters who met at Lloyd's found themselves writing something like nine-tenths of all the marine insurance business in the city.

Essentially this growing success was based on two things. First there was the law which had excluded the small companies. Second there was the ineffectiveness of the London Assurance and the Royal Exchange.

But there was a third point, almost as important—convenience. Before Lloyd's, and even in the early days of Tower Street, a broker could never be sure where he could find someone who would write a risk, or part of a risk, on a ship.

Now, with the increased standing of Lloyd's as a centre, he could be sure. And long before there was any kind of formal association, the Lombard Street coffee house had become what Lloyd's still is today: a market place where a broker can place his risk without going outside one building.

Beyond the narrow confines of the city other factors were also making for change. Maritime trade was expanding. New trading centres like Birmingham and Manchester needed outlets for their goods to go to the world. Britain had reached a pre-eminence in trade unparalleled since the days of Elizabeth. At Lloyd's in Lombard Street, the heady smell of success must have mingled with the aromatic scent of coffee.

Meanwhile at the coffee house itself there had been changes; the winter of 1712–13 seems to have been a fairly dramatic one in the Lloyd family. In the October, Edward Lloyd's second wife died, and the following month he had married his third wife, Martha. In January his daughter Handy had married her father's head waiter William Newton—possibly Newton had an eye to the main chance and his master's failing health, for two months after the wedding Edward Lloyd died.

Whatever Newton's motives, he did not enjoy the ownership of the coffee house for long. Within a year of Lloyd's death he himself was dead. Handy, following family tradition, got married again, this time to Samuel Shepherd, who remained master of the coffee house till 1727.

Shepherd was succeeded by Thomas Jemson, who deserves a place in any story of Lloyd's if only because it was during his time that *Lloyd's List* made its first appearance. Edward Lloyd himself, you may remember, had begun a newspaper of shipping news in 1696. *Lloyd's News* had survived for a year and then ceased publication. Possibly Jemson had seen a copy of the original *News*—or possibly he was simply catering for the growing need of his customers. In any case he brought out the first edition of the new paper in 1734. No copies earlier than 1740 have come down to us, but in that issue, there is a mention of the fact that from now on, instead of appearing weekly, it will be 'published every Tuesday and Friday. Subscriptions are taken at Three Shillings per Quarter, at the Bar of Lloyd's coffee house in Lombard Street.'

The new publication was clearly a good deal more professional than the somewhat rough-and-ready notes of ships' arrivals which Edward Lloyd had completed with the help of runners from Shadwell and Wapping or the gossip of ships' captains. By now Lloyd's must have already been beginning to build up its network of correspondents who, by the 1780s, would be sending lists of arrivals, sailings and casualties from all the British and Irish ports. Till the end of the eighteenth century the form of *Lloyd's List* would remain unchanged, with the solitary addition on the front page of the time of high water at London Bridge, 'taken from Mr Flamstead's correct Tide Table'.

Meanwhile, what about the actual business of insuring ships? The War of the Austrian Succession brought new hazards to the underwriters. Gibb writes that by the early 1740s 'the loss of our merchant tonnage was alarming . . . In the later stages of the war the losses became a good deal heavier for (according to *Lloyd's List*) two hundred and ninety-seven ships were captured in 1748, three hundred and seven in 1744, and in 1747 no less than four hundred and fifty-seven. And by far the greater part of the financial loss was carried by Lloyd's underwriters.'

Faced with this, there was not much the underwriters could do, except what a Lloyd's man would do in the same situation today—pay up as cheerfully as possible, and put up the premiums. At the same time, another more insidious threat was looming. This was the new attack of the gambling frenzy which had gripped the City in the 1710s.

At first sight it might seem unlikely that gambling should have had much to do with people whose job was marine insurance. But what we have to remember is that for much of the eighteenth century gambling was a kind of national addiction. Later in the century, Walpole wrote that young men of fashion would often lose £10,000 in an evening at the whist and faro banks of Brook's and Almack's.

Edward Gibbon once worked out Charles James Fox's gambling losses and calculated that over a period the Whig leader would lose around £500 an hour. Nor was the fever limited to addicts like Fox or a group of hell-raisers. Even so gentle and moral a character as William Wilberforce once decided he must curb his love of the tables, but even then he only made a resolution to limit his losses to £50 a session.

By the 1760s the contagion had spread to Lloyd's. In 1763 the coffee house had passed into the possession of one Thomas Lawrence, who seems to have been the weakest and least effective in the long succession of masters.

Whether Lawrence encouraged the gambling, or simply did not try to stop it, we do not know. But certainly by 1768 it was threatening Lloyd's whole reputation. It was possible to get a policy – which was a dignified way of saying a bet – on almost anything. You could get a policy on whether there would be a war with France or Spain, whether John Wilkes would be arrested or die in jail, or whether some Parliamentary candidate would be elected. Underwriters offered premiums of 25 per cent on George II's safe return from Dettingen; there were policies on whether this or that mistress of Louis XV would continue in favour or not.

One particularly grisly form of speculation, quoted by Thomas Mortimer in a book published in 1781 and engagingly entitled *The Mystery and Iniquity of Stock Jobbing*, was this:

> A practice likewise prevailed of insuring the lives of well-known personages as soon as a paragraph appeared in the newspapers, announcing them to be dangerously ill. The insurance rose in proportion as intelligence could be procured from the servants, or from any of the faculty attending, that the patient was in great danger. This inhuman sport affected the minds of men depressed by long sickness; for when such persons, casting an eye over a newspaper for amusement, saw that their lives had been insured in the Alley at 90 per cent, they despaired of all hopes; and thus their dissolution was hastened.

It is possible that at Lloyd's such activities were limited to a few. Even so, the whole reputation of the coffee house was endangered.

Fortunately for Lloyd's, a group of the more conscientious and far-sighted underwriters saw the danger. In 1769 they began negotiations with Thomas Fielding, one of Lawrence's waiters. The idea was that Fielding should set up a new establishment under the name of New Lloyd's Coffee House. Before the end of the year this breakaway group had found premises at Number 5, Pope's Head Alley.

For the next two years a sort of private warfare seems to have gone on between the old Lloyd's and the new. It was true that Lawrence still had the name and the facilities, which included the publication of *Lloyd's List* and the other shipping intelligence. It was also true that his premises were far better equipped than the Pope's Head Alley house, which was small, inconvenient and draughty. Indeed from the beginning the underwriters seem to have regarded it as little better than a staging post till they could find something better.

But Fielding's coffee house, for all its discomfort, drew the nucleus of the underwriters who had made Lloyd's. And this, in the event, was to be decisive.

For a while attacks and counter-attacks went on in the public announcements column of the press. Then gradually it became clear that the New Lloyd's group were gaining the ascendant. Before long they were publishing their own version of *Lloyd's List*. Inevitably, the business at Lombard Street began to dwindle.

Meanwhile the events of 1769 had been considerably more than a change of scene. What they implied above all was a movement by the underwriters themselves to determine their own future. Fielding as master of the coffee house had an important role, but it was no longer the key role it had been in the past. At the end of 1771 a group of seventy-nine underwriters and brokers set down what has been called the most important document in Lloyd's history: 'We the Underwritten do agree to pay our Several Subscriptions into the Bank of England in the Names of a Committee to be chosen by Ballot for the Building A New Lloyd's Coffee House.'

What was important was not simply the quest for a new building—it was that at last Lloyd's was operating as a group with a common interest. Nine years later when the committee published its first-ever List of Members, it was significantly entitled 'A List of Subscribers to Lloyd's *from the Foundation in 1771*'.

If 1771 is therefore the date for the beginning of the modern Lloyd's, the events of the next two years were hardly less important. From 1772 we have the first minute-books of the newly formed committee. In the following year we come to something else which is a Lloyd's landmark. This time it is not from Lloyd's own records, but from the minutes of a sub-committee of the Mercers' Company, the owners of the Royal Exchange: 'Mr Angurstine [*sic*] from the gentlemen who attend New Lloyd's Coffee house Attended to be informed if there was any large room to be lett over the Exchange. The Committee Ordered the Clerk with the Surveyor to let Mr Angurstine view the two Rooms late in lease to the British Fishery.'

The Clerk to the Sub-Committee of the Mercers' Company can be forgiven for not getting the right spelling of what must have seemed to him an unusual name. John Julius Angerstein was not, in 1773, even a member of the committee of Lloyd's.

On that day, however, something historic had happened. The underwriters and the brokers at Lloyd's had not merely found the new accommodation they were seeking. They had also found the man who, from then till the end of the century, was largely to shape their fortunes.

'Individually we are underwriters but collectively we are Lloyd's.' In one sense Lloyd's can be described as a loosely organized association of people with business interests in common, working together under a common roof.

But there the implication of equality ends. In the eighteenth century as now, Lloyd's depended on a few individuals far-sighted enough to see not merely the next step but the one beyond it.

In the Room today there are perhaps twenty underwriters who will lead a risk, knowing that the rest of the market will follow. This is not just a question of deciding to take a chance. Very often the kind of insurance they are writing will be something new, tailored to a special need, and the terms of it will have been hacked out in endless discussions between them and the broker. It is the sense of innovation which is at the heart of Lloyd's, and through the centuries it has been carried forward by a relatively few people.

The first of these – or the first of whom we have any knowledge – was John Julius Angerstein. The son of a German family who had emigrated to Russia, he was born in St Petersburg in 1735. Sent to London at the age of fourteen, he had served his apprenticeship in the counting house of a merchant – presumably a friend of his father's – who dealt with Russia. From there he had moved to Lloyd's where he had found his true *métier* in the world of marine insurance.

When you look at the portrait of Angerstein which hangs in the Nelson Room at Lloyd's today, you have the sense of a natural aristocrat of commerce. There is shrewdness in the face, worldliness and a certain disdain. It is not exactly arrogant, but you feel that it is not the face of a man who would have suffered fools gladly. If he had little time for fools, he had still less for knaves. Once, many years later, he was questioned about the presence in the Room of some unsavoury underwriters' clerks who were in the habit of writing risks on which they had no money to pay losses.

'I cannot speak to it,' said Angerstein with weary disdain. 'I do not know their names.' One senses a contempt which was not only on moral grounds. The wider contempt was for those who did not see Lloyd's, as he did, as a great instrument of commerce.

Angerstein was chairman of Lloyd's from 1790 to 1796, and in those days he was a nationally known figure, both as the financial adviser to William Pitt and as a patron of the arts whose private collection would later become the nucleus of the National Gallery.

Long before he became chairman, it is safe to assume, he had been a dominating figure. Slips on which he had written a line were known as Julians, after his second Christian name. Angerstein gave a lead, the rest of the market would follow—just as more than a century later, when non-marine insurance began, the market would follow C. E. Heath.

As a broker, Angerstein placed the largest insurance then ever written at Lloyd's, for £656,800 on the treasure carried from Vera Cruz to England on a frigate called the *Diana*. Often he dealt in risks which must have at the time seemed both frightening and novel. In 1794, Lloyd's underwriters lost hundreds of thousands of pounds on Dutch and Russian ships seized by hostile governments in the Napoleonic War. Angerstein, quick to try to convert a huge loss to a potential profit, bought the salvage rights. 'Two years afterwards,' writes Gibb, 'the losses were repaid to underwriters and Angerstein's speculation proved profitable. (It was) the first recorded case of an underwriter speculating on the prospects of salvage after payment of a total loss!'

But in 1773 all this was in the future. At the time of his visit to the Mercers' Company Angerstein was only thirty-eight, an insurance broker with an office of his own in Old Broad Street.

From all the records it seems that the attempt to get the Royal Exchange rooms was his own idea. Angerstein had been one of the group which had originally headed the move to Pope's Head Alley, but at this stage he was not even a member of the newly formed Lloyd's Committee.

To a young man bursting with initiative and the sort of ranging far-sightedness which is part of his legacy to Lloyd's, the procrastinations of the Committee may well have been irritating. One can imagine his getting to hear of the two rooms 'late in lease to the British Fishery' and deciding to do something about it. At any rate, he seems to have taken matters into his own hands. He called a meeting of the members of Lloyd's, got their authority to proceed, and negotiated the lease of the rooms in his own name. On 16 November 1773 he and three other subscribers signed it 'for themselves and the rest of the Committee for New Lloyd's Coffee House' for twenty-one years at a rent of £160 a year.

Like the move to Pope's Head Alley, this second move to the Royal Exchange was much more than simply a change of location. In a particular sense it meant – and it is a point that seems worth saluting – the end of the coffee house. For three-quarters of a century marine insurance in London had been tied to the idea of the coffee house. Miraculously, it had survived and prospered. When one comes to think of it, it is a little as if cricket had survived because of the existence of the Tavern at Lord's or as if Eton had only kept going because of its tuck shop.

It was a debt of which Angerstein and his fellow members were well aware. Even when the Lloyd's market opened for the first time at the Royal Exchange on 5 March 1774, the main rooms were described as 'Coffee Rooms', and indeed coffee continued to be served in them. There were regulations about no sedan chairs being brought in. One innovation was a Loss and Arrival Book exhibited in the subscribers' room, which was kept for the members only, and was guarded by one of the waiters. Otherwise the scenery was much the same. There was still the pulpit which the Kidney would mount to declaim important news. The boxes, as you can see from Plate 7, were ranged round the walls in much the same way as they had been in Lombard Street.

One other point was significant. Just before the move from Pope's Head Alley the subscribers came to an arrangement with Thomas Fielding who had been, you may remember, Master of the coffee house in Pope's Head Alley. It was arranged that Fielding should go with them to the Royal Exchange, and should take his head waiter, Thomas Taylor, into partnership. Fielding and Taylor were to take the profits from the sale of coffee, and there were various arrangements made by the subscribers for payments to be made to Fielding's wife in the event of his death.

In other words the masters were now the servants. The underwriters and brokers were no longer mere frequenters of a coffee house.

They were now the subscribers of Lloyd's, and what they had achieved was the ground-plan of the modern market.

3
Unlimited Liability

'It's very nice to welcome you here.'

'It's very nice to be here.'

'We'd just like to ask you,' says the Chairman of the Rota Committee, 'one or two questions. We are here as representatives of the Committee of Lloyd's. We'd like to make certain of one or two things.'

The candidate, who happens to be Irish, nods and says he quite understands. As well he might, for over the last few weeks he will have been carefully briefed about this meeting. The object of the Rota Committee is to make a final check on the credentials of anyone who is applying to join a syndicate—to become what is known at Lloyd's, a little mysteriously, as a Name.

'We'd like to be quite sure you've had things explained to you.' The Chairman is in his middle forties, a quiet, courteous man with an air of authority which he tends to play down. 'You know what is meant by Unlimited Liability?'

The candidate nods, rather seriously this time, and says he does understand.

'We like to make sure about that. Down to your last shirt button.' The Chairman grins amiably. So do the rest of the three-man committee. Unlimited Liability is something Lloyd's men like making jokes about, rather in the same way it is said that only really religious people can make jokes about God.

'And you've also understood about the control of your funds being in the hands of your underwriting agent? The point is it can make life rather difficult for an underwriter if he feels you're breathing down his neck.'

The Irishman says he can quite see that, and the underwriting agent who is here as his sponsor nods. If he hadn't explained that to his candidate, he says, he wouldn't have been doing his job very well. There is another general laugh. All the same, the Irishman looks round the room with a certain awe. With its chandeliers and Adam fireplace, the Committee Room of Lloyd's must be one of the most spectacular rooms in London. The candidate has flown over for this meeting especially from Dublin, and you feel it is an important day for him, a bit like being taken to a new school by your parents.

'And you've read the terms of the agreement between you and the underwriting agent?' After this come a few more general questions about whether the candidate has altered his financial arrangements since he completed his application. Everything seems to be in order, and the Chairman looks up.

'Well. I think that's all we want to ask you. Was there anything you want to ask us?'

It seems the Irishman has no questions; the Chairman shuffles his papers and looks up. 'Thank you *very* much. I do hope all goes well for you.' The expression sounds not merely formal—you feel he really likes the candidate and hopes he will succeed. The Irishman thanks them and goes out, then the mahogany door opens again.

This time they all get up—the candidate is a girl in her thirties, an attractive blonde in a red coat. There is an atmosphere of restrained gallantry—Lloyd's has only been admitting women for the last three years, and for the Committee, you feel, the experience is still novel.

After the Chairman has done the initial courtesies they sit down. 'Mrs May, isn't it? I believe you've come up from Kent today?'

Mrs May says she has, and the Chairman says he hopes the weather wasn't too bad. They'd had somebody else from Kent who had got stuck on the motorway because of the weather.

Mrs May says that must have been the other side of Kent, they had a lot of snow last night in the Weald.

'Oh, that's good.' The Chairman seems really relieved, then gets down to looking at her papers. 'Now the proposal here is that you're going to write £30,000 non-marine business with the Heath syndicate. And on the marine side up to £20,000 with Chester's. Have you met the underwriters who'll be handling your money?'

Mrs May says that she has just had lunch with them, and they were charming.

'I think that's very important.' The Chairman nods approvingly. 'After all, they've got your underwriting fate under their pens.'

Next comes the question about Unlimited Liability. Mrs May says she'd been told what it means and she understands it.

'It's not a thing to be taken lightly,' says the Chairman. 'We like to make sure you understand what it means. The only things you really need to know about Lloyd's,' he says, and everybody laughs, 'are Unlimited Liability and the Lutine Bell.'

There are a few more questions, then they get up. Lloyd's has demonstrated, if further demonstration were needed, its sense of style. Afterwards the Chairman says to me that it's not always easy to keep the right balance between the dignified and the informal, but they do their best. 'We like to make it an occasion people can remember,' he says. 'So much of life is retrospect or looking forward. It's good to recognize a moment that means something.'

Beyond this, what has also been demonstrated is Lloyd's huge integrity. But what really is Unlimited Liability, and how does it work?

Lloyd's concern with its own history is not merely narcissistic. Almost everything you see in the modern market is the result of a long, slow process. What has been built up over three hundred years is not simply the practice of how it works, but a set of principles. At the heart of these lies Unlimited Liability—the underwriter's obligation to pay on his losses.

In 1720, you remember, the private insurers of London were made personally liable for everything they had guaranteed to an assured person—the whole of their accumulated premiums, the law said, were to be made available to meet his claims. Over the years the principle had not always worked. Through the eighteenth century there had been many cases of underwriters failing to pay up.

On the other hand there had been instances – and they must have seemed remarkable in the free-for-all financial climate of those days – when the underwriters paid a claim as a matter of principle rather than because the law made them do so. In 1811 Angerstein could say of the underwriters at Lloyd's:

> I have known them to pay a loss where the merchant has made a mistake, and called it ship instead of goods, or goods instead of ship, and the underwriter, knowing it, took no advantage, and paid the loss; these are facts from my books. I have known a ship insured from one place to Europe, when she came from another, and that has been paid . . .

But this did not mean there was any absolute guarantee that the underwriter would pay up. He was bound to do so by law, and if he was an honest man he was also bound by honour. But there were many loopholes, and the Committee of Lloyd's had not, as yet, the power to close them.

According to Gibb, even by 1850

> an underwriting member could fail to pay his liabilities, could make a composition with his creditors, could even pass through the bankruptcy court, and still use the Room for broking and underwriting without any interference from the Committee. The Committee had no power to act, and its only course in dealing with a broken-down underwriter was to tell the door-keeper not to let the man pass the barrier . . . If any insolvent underwriter had had the physical strength to barge through the barricade or the moral determination to take action at law against the Committee, nothing

apparently could have prevented him from continuing to subscribe any policy that was offered to him.

But gradually, through those middle years of the nineteenth century, things were beginning to alter. In 1851 the Committee passed a bye-law that if a member became bankrupt he should be expelled from Lloyd's. Six years later, almost by chance, they accepted the first deposit against insolvency made by a new member.

True, the deposit was not sought by the Committee. It seems to have arisen simply because a certain Mr Sharp wanted to make his son an underwriting member and in those days it was conventional for the sponsor to guarantee that the person he was introducing would pay his debts. For some reason Mr Sharp had an objection on principle to giving such a guarantee. He asked the Committee if they would, instead, accept a deposit of £5,000 to meet any debts that his son might incur.

The Committee of Lloyd's do not seem to have regarded Mr Sharp's idea as particularly important, but they accepted it, and the acceptance became a precedent. By the beginning of the 1860s, though there was still no rule about it, anyone becoming an underwriting member of Lloyd's produced a deposit. By 1866 the process had become ratified—in cases where the Committee required a cash deposit, there had to be a Deed of Trust.

Even now, the Committee were still far from seeing themselves as in any way responsible for an underwriter's actions. In 1855, an underwriter named Gibson went bankrupt, and one of his creditors in Liverpool wrote to the Committee to ask them if they would see that a claim on his syndicate was paid. The Committee replied that they had no power to interfere. It was not in their province, they said, to discuss the subject; they were 'simply a Committee for managing the affairs of the establishment of Lloyd's'.

In other words, the process was not complete—there were

still gaps in the net of total security which Lloyd's was gradually weaving. The old tradition was still that it was a broker's job to distinguish between an underwriter who would pay his claims and an underwriter who would not. If he failed the Committee could now exclude him from the Room. But the Committee were not responsible beyond that, and so the situation went on till the end of the century. Then quite suddenly in 1903 something happened to change it. An underwriter named Burnand failed badly. The cause of his failure was that he had been running a travel agency as well as an underwriting syndicate.

Among other things Burnand had invested heavily in selling seats for the Coronation of King Edward VII. The Coronation had been postponed because of the King's illness, and the travel agency had lost its money. In an attempt to prop it up, he borrowed money from the banks, on the guarantee that his underwriting syndicate would insure the travel agency against any failure to meet their bills. What he had done, in effect, was to make his names responsible for debts amounting to £100,000, though most of them knew nothing about it.

In the event, Burnand himself was jailed, and four of his names were ruined. The incident was a storm signal for Lloyd's, but it was not the only one. In another case, an underwriter had borrowed money for his deposit from a friend, and paid his friend back from the premiums earned, so that when the claims came in there was no money to pay them.

Clearly the reputation of Lloyd's demanded some sort of action by the Committee. But given the nature of Lloyd's, what sort of action could they take? The whole point of Lloyd's as an insurance market had always been that it was not a company, but a collection of individuals. On the other hand, what was clearly needed was some form of direct control by the Committee. Slowly, and after much argument, they began to evolve the idea which was to become the corner-stone of their reputation in the twentieth century.

Put very simply, the idea was in two parts. First there would have to be what could be called a Premium Trust Fund, approved by the Committee, in which underwriters would be compelled to place their premiums. In this way no underwriter could take his profits until he knew what claims were going to be made against him. At the end of a set period he would be able to take the profits, but by then he would have lodged further premiums—there would consequently be a balance in the Trust Fund. Meanwhile the profits would have to be certified by the Committee of Lloyd's before any shares in them could be handed out to the names.

But the idea of certifying the profits implied something else—and the something else, in terms of Lloyd's history, was a revolution. It implied that the Committee would have to see the books of each underwriting syndicate, would have to act, in fact, as an auditor. In 1908 Lloyd's appointed a special committee to examine the possibility of setting up a new checking system.

From the beginning this was designed as far more than a mere accounting procedure. The Audit, as it began to be called, was designed to detect, at the first possible moment, any weakness in the financial structure of a syndicate. It would have the power to set a limit on the volume of business that any underwriter might write, according to the capital provided by his names.

Not surprisingly, the idea was not entirely acceptable to all the Edwardian individualists of Lloyd's; in November 1908 there was still doubt whether the procedure which the special committee had drawn up would be agreed to. But in 1908, as 150 years earlier, Lloyd's had its men of vision.

Just as Angerstein and his friends had seen the need to break clear of the gambling underwriters in the 1760s, so there was now a group of leading underwriters who saw what needed to be done. Prominent among them was Cuthbert Heath, the man who, in the 1880s, had written Lloyd's first non-marine insurance policy. Among the most treasured possessions of

Lloyd's today is a piece of foolscap paper on which forty leading underwriters some time had signed their names to a few words in Heath's handwriting: 'We the undersigned underwriting Members, would agree to hand in to the Committee of Lloyd's annually a statement signed by an approved accountant that we were in possession of assets reasonably sufficient to wind up our underwriting accounts.'

For a scrap of paper, its influence was to be immense. Once Heath and the other leaders had come out in favour of it, the issue was no longer in doubt.

By March 1909 the members of Lloyd's submitted themselves to the Annual Audit for the first time, and the modern history of Lloyd's had begun.

With the coming of the Audit the Committee of Lloyd's assumed a new role. Without interference in the actual running of individual syndicates, they had now set up a means of control whose object was to protect the public and preserve Lloyd's reputation. Even so, as events were to show, they had not yet gone far enough.

It is one of the striking things about the story of Lloyd's that whenever there has been trouble it has always been followed by a deft move to put Lloyd's house in order. When Angerstein and his friends saw the reputation of the coffee house threatened by the gambling underwriters of the 1760s, they took rapid action to shed them. When the Committee saw how Burnand had found it possible to convert his names' money, they invented the Premium Trust Fund and the Audit.

In 1923 the Committee found themselves in similar, but much worse, trouble. This time it was caused by an underwriter named Harrison, whose business was in the non-marine market, and who specialized in motor insurance. Among his clients were several companies involved in the then novel business of selling cars on hire purchase.

In order to provide working capital for themselves, the

hire-purchase companies borrowed money from discount houses. The security they offered was in the form of bills signed by the hire-purchasers. Thus, if someone failed to complete his payments, the bill meant that there would be at least a second-hand car to dispose of. If the bills were also covered by an insurance policy which guaranteed credit of the purchaser, it made the deal that much more solid-looking from the point of view of the discount houses who were going to lend the money.

Increasingly, Harrison began to deal in this kind of insurance—credit insurance, as it is known. By early 1923 he had guaranteed more than £2 million worth of bills, often knowing nothing of the true state of credit of the person they were drawn on.

It was not long before there came the first ominous sound of Harrison's impending crash. One of his credit risks was a man named Holsteinson, a Swedish citizen living in London, whose business was owning fleets of coaches and taxis. At least he claimed to own them—probably some at least of the taxis and coaches were real. The rest was imaginary. Holsteinson had invented registrations and engine numbers, on the strength of which the optimistic Harrison had guaranteed his bills of credit. Some time during the spring of 1923 Holsteinson disappeared.

Harrison found himself owing the discount brokers £17,000 on a fleet of fictitious taxis.

It is conceivable that if Harrison had admitted his follies to the Committee of Lloyd's, the result would have been no worse than a ban on his future underwriting. But there was something else which Harrison could not admit to the Committee. This was that he had been keeping two sets of books, one which he submitted to the Audit, and another which reported his true dealings.

All that summer Harrison went on writing more and more policies in a blind attempt to extricate himself from his troubles. Meanwhile the Audit sub-committee had begun to scent something wrong. They had already asked for more money to be paid into his names' Trust Funds. Then, in October 1923, the bank refused to honour one of his cheques. Harrison was asked to produce his true accounts to the Chairman of Lloyd's, A. L. Sturge. When Sturge examined them, he found the amount owing to the discount brokers was in the region of £200,000.

The importance of the Harrison case lies not in the re-telling of the story of a pathetic fraud, but in what followed. Within eight days of Harrison's confession, Sturge had been through the books, called a meeting of the Committee and laid the facts before them.

When they understood the situation, Sturge said one thing to them, and what he said was historic. He told them that Harrison's debts would have to be met by the other members of Lloyd's. He had no authority to say it, and that in a sense makes what he told them more impressive. It was the expression, perhaps the most complete expression, of Lloyd's integrity.

Before the Committee meeting broke up on that October afternoon, Sturge's view had been accepted. Harrison's debts were to be charged on every member of Lloyd's, in proportion to their premium income. When the underwriters paid their shares, the amount varied from £10,000 to eightpence. The members of Lloyd's had not only demonstrated the truth of the old description that individually they were underwriters but collectively they were Lloyd's—they had given it a new force. From 1923 onwards, a Lloyd's policy carried a guarantee of liability far beyond that which any conventional insurance company has ever offered; greater indeed, than some conventional insurance companies offer to this day.

It remained to secure the last loopholes. Soon after the Harrison case, the whole hazardous field of credit insurance was completely barred by the Committee of Lloyd's. In 1924 it became compulsory for all policies to be issued through the Policy Signing Office, which would bring a new means of tighter control. An additional fund called the Central Fund was set up to cover any possible future defaults by an underwriter who might find a means, as Harrison had done, to cheat the Audit, or for that matter an underwriter who quite genuinely could not pay his debts. This fund – today it stands at many millions of pounds, though Lloyd's has never disclosed the exact figure – was to be made up from contributions from all members of Lloyd's, in proportion to their premium income.

Thus the safety net was now complete, and the principle of Unlimited Liability established. How does this affect the individual underwriter today? It is time now to look at what an underwriter really does, and what we mean by a syndicate.

One of the things they are fond of quoting at Lloyd's is an Elizabethan definition of insurance—'by means of whiche it comethe to passe that upon the losse or perishinge of any shippe there followethe not the undoinge of any man, but the losse lighteth reather easilie upon many than heavilie upon few.'

Obviously this principle of spreading the load works in the sense of various underwriters taking a line or percentage on a risk. On what is always called the hull of a ship or a jet aircraft, for instance, even the most heavily involved underwriter will usually take only about 7 per cent.

But this is only the first stage of spreading the load. Obviously not all the 7 per cent is the underwriter's own money. He writes his line as representative of a syndicate. There are about 250 syndicates in the Room of Lloyd's—114 marine, 75 non-marine, and about 30 each for motor insurance and aviation. Mrs May, you remember, was going to write her marine insurance with Chester's. Thinking it might be useful to see who was actually going to be handling her money, I rang up Mr Henry Chester and explained that I was writing a book about Lloyd's and asked if we could meet and have a talk.

Mr Chester said he'd be delighted. He and the two other underwriters on his syndicate always met for coffee in the

Captains' Room at ten-fifteen, and would I care to join them? The Captains' Room, a sort of inner club within the club-like atmosphere of Lloyd's, is virtually an enshrinement of the spirit of the coffee house. When I got there the room was full of small parties of underwriters and brokers sitting discussing the forthcoming day's business under the portraits of past chairmen.

Henry Chester turned out to be a dark, serious-looking man with a trenchant way of talking and a slightly brooding kind of deadpan humour. He introduced the other two underwriters, Geoffrey Welch who specializes in excess loss accounts and aviation, and Tom Poole who looks after cargoes and goods in transit, including livestock.

I asked Tom Poole what sort of livestock they usually were and he said that depended, it could be anything from dolphins to Mill Reef. He'd had a lot of dolphins travelling the previous day, he said, from Florida to Berlin, wrapped in foam rubber.

Henry Chester said you wouldn't think foam rubber would be enough, you'd think they'd need to have a bath somewhere between Florida and Berlin. Tom Poole agreed, but said that seemed to be the way they usually travelled. 'Not that you could make a living,' he said as if to get things into perspective, 'out of writing dolphins. About once a year I write a crocodile. It's rather fun.'

After we'd disposed of the dolphins, I asked them what sort of things they usually talked about at their morning meeting. They said it depended, which is one of the things Lloyd's people are fond of saying as if they rather pride themselves on the fact that nothing is done by rules. Sometimes, Henry Chester said, they might just talk about last night's programme on the telly. On the other hand there might be a particular question they needed to think over in a relaxed way and not in the fairly hectic atmosphere of the box, where they spend most of the day. 'From time to time we'll stop writing a class of business. We might say we're going to start writing a new sort, and discuss the implications. We might talk about a problem that a particular broker's brought up the day before.'

Tom Poole said one of the things he needed to discuss with the other two some time was a rather complicated claim from somebody whose factory had been burnt down in Australia, it was thought because of arson. The matter had got to be discussed with the other underwriters involved. It seemed some of the others might want to invoke some sort of escape-clause called a right of recourse. Tom Poole, on the other hand, thought they'd have to pay up.

'It seems to me,' he said, 'we've got to get the other underwriters to compromise. You can't expect a man to risk having his factory burnt down by some disgruntled employee.'

Henry Chester asked if he thought they would agree, and Geoffrey Welch said he thought so. Chester nodded and said, suddenly rather seriously, that they'd have to try to get a compromise of some sort. 'At the end of the day we're Lloyd's men. Over something like this we shall act in unison.'

After coffee I said we hadn't got on to what I really wanted to ask them, which was about the syndicate. Henry Chester said this would be easier to explain if I'd like to come over to the office. Not all syndicates have offices in Lloyd's building: some of the very large ones have offices in some other building close by, so that their actual foothold in Lloyd's building is only the few square feet taken up by their box in the Room. H. G. Chester & Co. have three quite small offices on the fifth floor with rather splendid oak doors and their name in white letters.

Henry Chester's own room turned out to be the smallest of the three, with not much in the way of furniture except a desk and filing cabinet and a picture of an oil rig on the wall. Spread over the desk were about seven sheets of paper, covered with a gigantic long-division sum that trailed over from one sheet to the next like a serial. He explained that these were some figures for the Chairman of Lloyd's who was making a speech that afternoon and needed some statistics on the marine underwriting market. Chester had spent most of the morning before coffee doing this particular sum, and it still wasn't right yet, somewhere.

After he had shunted the long-division sum out of the way he got out a large paper-backed book which was called *Lloyd's Underwriting Syndicates* and spread it on the desk. The first thing I had to understand, he said, was that H. G. Chester was really two firms. First, it was a syndicate of underwriters with unlimited liability. Second, it was an underwriting *agency*. It was a limited liability company which ran the underwriting agency.

I said this all seemed rather involved and he agreed. 'If you look in the *Syndicates* book,' he said, 'you'll find the name of H. G. Chester about seventeen times. The first reference is to H. G. Chester and Others, which is the syndicate. The next one is to H. G. Chester Ltd, which is the underwriting agency. The next nine references are to sub-agencies which don't themselves write marine business but whose names are farmed out to us. Conversely, if one of our names wants to write fire business or motor, then we farm him out to one of the syndicates which handle them.'

'This was why Mrs May came to you for marine business?'

'Yes. You remember she was primarily a name with Heath, which is a non-marine syndicate. She wanted to spread her risk over marine as well, so Heath's passed her on to us. Our own syndicate consists of fifty names—but in addition to that, I'm writing marine business for another 220 names on other syndicates.'

I said I thought I'd got that, and we went on to look at the list of names on Chester's own syndicate. Opposite each name was written a figure, for example 20 or 100. Each of these, Henry Chester said, represented £1,000—thus the person with 20 opposite his name was prepared to write up to £20,000.

Before anyone can be a name at Lloyd's, he went on to

explain, he now has to pass a Means Test. This means he has to show the Committee of Lloyd's that he has a minimum of £75,000 in capital. In addition to this, he must lodge his deposit – nowadays the minimum is £10,000 – with the Committee. The amount of premium the name is allowed to write is geared to his deposit. The minimum is £8,000, but the amount is more likely to be in the region of £40,000.

Then where, I asked, did unlimited liability come in? If the underwriter made a heavy loss, didn't the name just lose his deposit?

'Not at all, that's the whole point. It's not just like buying shares on the Stock Market. If you have shares in a company and it goes bust, you lose your money. If you put your money in a Lloyd's syndicate and it goes bust, you could lose everything. First of all the Committee of Lloyd's will take all the money you've got in your underwriting account at the moment. If that isn't enough they'll take your bank account. Finally they'll take your deposit. I've never known anyone actually lose the shirt off their back, but I've known chaps,' he said cheerfully, 'who've had to sell their house and move into a bungalow. That's about the worse I've ever known happen.'

Even so, I said, unlimited liability seemed a daunting thought. I asked what the underwriter himself might expect to lose in a bad year? Henry Chester said rather ruefully that the worst years they'd had were 1965–68. They had been in a bit of a trough anyway, before that, and then there had come a couple of American hurricanes to clinch it—Hurricane Betsy had gone right up the Mississippi and ripped into a whole lot of ships that the syndicate had written. In those two years the syndicate hadn't sent the names their annual cheque—it had to ask them each for £4,000. He himself had lost £24,000 though mostly not on his own syndicate. 'It wasn't exactly the moment I'd have chosen, because we'd got kids at school and there was a credit squeeze on. All the same, we stood it.'

It occurred to me that an underwriter must do pretty well

the rest of the time to face up to losses like these, and he agreed. 'If you've got the cash to start with and you have got the right underwriting agent, you can do very nicely—anyone writing up to £50,000 can make £5,000 in a year. You're allowed to write a multiple of your deposit, and you're using the money twice—because the Committee of Lloyd's don't invest your deposit for themselves, they pay you the dividend. Even so it's the worst thing in the world for a worrier. We do occasionally get the sort of name who will hear that some ship's gone down, and they'll ring up to see if we've had a line on it. On the whole, though, they're a minority—the names leave us to get on with it, and it's important that they do. That's why, at the Rota Committee, they ask everyone if they've understood that the underwriter has total responsibility for handling their money.'

What, I asked, was the real skill of underwriting? Henry Chester thought for a bit and said it was a mistake to suppose, as most people did, that the worst thing that could happen to an underwriter was a shipwreck or an earthquake: in a sense, he said, they thrived on trouble. If there was a loss, it meant they would simply put the rates up. 'If you've done your sums right, you wouldn't be affected by the QE2 going down. It'd make a hole in your profits but it wouldn't worry you. Where you do go wrong is when your premium levels are wrong. Nowadays repairing costs are going up so fast that the difficulty we're all in is to know where to set the rate for a risk.' (Later I asked another underwriter the same question and he said it was a bit like being a racing driver. He quoted the example of Fangio, who was said to have calculated the exact speed that was right for every racetrack. 'He'd decide on his speed for the course and stick to it, whatever happened to everyone else. If he'd got his speed right he'd overtake people who were too slow and the people who tried to go round faster would blow up. In the same way if you get your premium-rate right, you won't be hit by losses.')

Coming back to the syndicate, I asked, What would happen

if somebody wanted to become an underwriter and he didn't happen to have £75,000 lying around?

Henry Chester stressed that Lloyd's was nowadays much more democratic. His own guess was that about half the underwriters nowadays had come up from being clerks in the Room. In this case, the syndicates that employ them would put up the deposits. On Henry Chester's box there are ten people apart from the three underwriters, and half of them have been made members. In the case of a Lloyd's man, the deposit is reduced to £8,000 and there is no Means Test. 'From the syndicate's point of view,' he said, 'it's worth it because it repays their loyalty.'

There was one other thing, I said, which I hadn't asked about, and that was the Audit. Apart from the pages of the long-division sum, there didn't seem much in the way of accounting going on. Henry Chester said this was all done by a firm of outside accountants they shared with another syndicate.

'All the same I can give you an idea,' he said, going over to one of the filing cabinets. 'These are our cargo accounts for 1969. All our accounts have to go rather a long way back, because we've got to allow for claims to come in. But in 1969 we made £734,000 in premiums and paid out £619,000 in claims. Those figures go to the Audit Committee of Lloyd's, and their requirement was £55,000.'

'How do they arrive at £55,000?'

'That's the figure worked out by the Audit Department and the accountants. Virtually you can say it's an amount which gives you a safe leeway. There could conceivably be more than that amount of claims on the risks we wrote in 1969—but if there were, there'd be other resources to meet them.' He did yet another sum on one of the pieces of paper. 'If you take 619 and 55 from 734 you get 60. So £60,000's our profit on the cargo account once we've been through the Audit.'

After a bit Henry Chester started eyeing the pages of his long-division sum and said he really ought to be getting on

1

The Room at Lloyd's.

The Lutine Bell. Lloyd's most historic symbol, it is nowadays rarely rung except on important occasions.

2

3

John Julius Angerstein and his wife, painted by Sir Thomas Lawrence. Angerstein's interest in painting was reflected by the fact that his own collection formed the nucleus of the National Gallery.

Some of the plate presented to Nelson after the Battle of the Nile. 'We are all obliged,' wrote Nelson to the Committee of Lloyd's, 'by your humane attention to us seamen.'

4

5

The position of Caller is one of the direct survivals of the coffee house. Walter Farrant, *left*, was a famous Caller in Victorian times. In the modern Room, *below*, the Caller's function is to relay the names of brokers.

6

7

The coffee house in the eighteenth century (*above*). The sketch below is of a reconstruction produced for the Montreal Exhibition. Note the Caller's pulpit, and the boxes in the foreground.

8

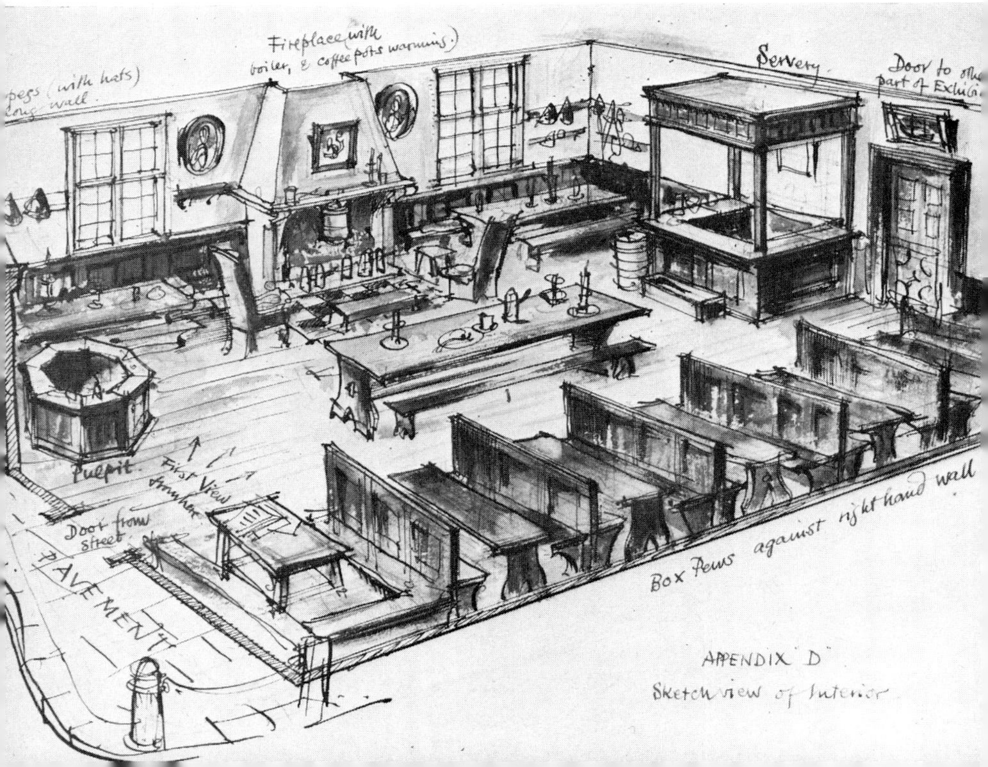

9

The Royal Exchange in the eighteenth century. When Lloyd's moved into the building with the Stock Exchange, it was described as 'the Palladium of commerce'.

The nineteenth-century Room and, *right*, a waiter. Even today, uniformed staff are known as waiters, and wear the traditional scarlet coat and velvet collar.

10

11

LLOYD's LIST. N° 560.

FRIDAY, January 2. 1740.

THIS List, which was formerly publish'd once a Week, will now continue to be publish'd every *Tuesday* and *Friday*, with the Addition of the Stocks Course of Exchange, *&c.*——Subscriptions are taken in at Three Shillings per Quarter, at the Bar of *Lloyd*'s Coffee-House in *Lombard-Street*.

Such Gentlemen as are willing to encourage this Undertaking, shall have them carefully deliver'd according to their Directions.

London *Exchanges* on	
Amst.	34 11 a 10
Ditto Sight	34 $7\frac{1}{2}$ a 8
Rott.	35 a 1
Antw.	35 11 a 36
Hamb:	33 10 2U a 11 $2\frac{1}{2}$
Paris —	$32\frac{5}{8}$
Ditto at 2U	$32\frac{3}{8}$
Bourdeaux a Usance	$32\frac{5}{8}$
Cadiz —	$42\frac{5}{8}$
Madrid	$42\frac{5}{8}$
Bilboa	$41\frac{5}{8}$
Leghorn	$51\frac{1}{4}$
Genoa	55
Venice	$51\frac{3}{4}$
Lisbon	5 $4\frac{7}{8}$ a 5
Oporto	5 $4\frac{1}{2}$
Dublin	8

Aids in the Exchequer		*Given for*	*Paid off*
18th 2 Shilling	1739	1000000	926800
18th 4 Ditto	1740	2000000	482600
Malt——	1739	750000	501014
Salt——	1734	1000000	910500

Gold in Coin - - - -	3	18	1
Ditto in Barrs - - -	3	18	
Ps of Eight: Pillar large - - -	0	5	7 $\frac{1}{2}$
Ditto Small - -	0	5	6 $\frac{1}{2}$
Mexico large - -	0	5	7 $\frac{1}{2}$
Ditto Small - -	0	5	6 $\frac{5}{8}$
Silver in Barrs - - -	0	5	7 $\frac{5}{8}$

(per Oz)

Annuities.

14*l.* per Cent at $22\frac{1}{2}$ Years Purchase

1704 to 1708 Inclusive $24\frac{1}{2}$ ditto

$3\frac{1}{2}$ per Cent. 1 per Cent. præm.

3 per Cent. $5\frac{1}{4}$ Disc.

Cochineal 20s 0d per. lb. *Discount* 00s per Cent.

Lottery 1710.

Prizes for 3 Years from *Michaelmas* last are in course of Payment

Blanks for 3 Years from *Michaelmas* last 1l. 10s *per* Set.

—*Price* of **Stocks**.—	*Wednesday*	*Thursday*	*Friday*
Bank Stock - - - - -	$138\frac{1}{2}$ a $\frac{3}{4}$		$138\frac{1}{2}$
East India- - - - - - - -		156	156 a $56\frac{1}{4}$
South Sea - - - - -	$98\frac{3}{4}$		$98\frac{3}{4}$
Ditto Anuity Old	$110\frac{1}{4}$ a 10	$110\frac{5}{8}$	$110\frac{5}{8}$
Ditto——New	$110\frac{3}{8}$ a $\frac{1}{4}$	$110\frac{1}{4}$	$110\frac{1}{4}$
3 *per* Cent. Annuity 1726 - 1731			$99\frac{1}{4}$
Million Bank - - -	113	113	113
Equivalent - - - - - -	112	112	112
R. Ass. 100l paid in			
L: Ass. 13l paid in	$10\frac{3}{4}$	$10\frac{1}{4}$	$10\frac{3}{4}$
7 per Cent Em. Loan	98	98	98
5 per Cent. Ditto	$74\frac{3}{4}$	$74\frac{3}{4}$	75
Bank Circulation	2l 10s 0d	2l 10s 0d	2l 10s 0d
Lottery Tickets	5l 16s 0d	5l 17s 0d	6l 00s 0d

India Transfer Books open the 19th of January

Royal Assurance the 20th of January

South Sea New Annuity the 22d of January, 3 per Cent Annuities the 21st and 22d of January

South Sea Stock the 4th of February

The 5 per Cent Emperor's Loan, sells as above without the six Months Interest of 2 and a quarter per Cent, and 5 per Cent. part of the Principal to be paid of both, are now paying at the Bank

The India Dividend will be paid the 29th of January, South Sea New Annuities the 29th ditto, and the S. Sea Stock the 6th and 7th of February,

Navy and Victualling Bills to the 30th June last are in course of Payment.

—*Interest per Cent*	*Wednesday*	*Thursday*	*Friday*	
3 India Bonds new	79	80	80	Shill: Præms
4 Salt Tallies	$\frac{1}{4}$ a $\frac{3}{8}$	$\frac{1}{4}$ a $\frac{5}{8}$	$\frac{1}{4}$ a $\frac{3}{8}$	

The MARINE LIST.

	Gravesend ——	Arrived from
30	Dec. Draper, Leach	Dublin
	Katherine, Roberts	Figuera
	Globe, Harvey	Lisbon
	Expedition, Major	Gibralter
1	Industry, Sheppardson	Virginia
	Leostoff	arrived from
	Swedish Liberty, Vischer	Stockholm
	Harwich ——	arrived from
	Success, Hartley	Gottenburg
	Liverpool ——	*arrived from*
	Dove, Drinkwater	Virginia
	Leopard, ——	ditto
	Bristol ——	*arrived from*
31	Elizabeth, Cheshire	Antigua
	Penzance	Arrived from
	Anne Sloop, Mitchel	Maderia
	Falmouth ——	*Arrived* from
27	Cleve, Rice	London
		Sailed for
	Mary Galley, Cross	Gibralter
	Dartmouth ——	Arrived from
28	Greenwich, ——	London
	Faulker, ——	N.foundland
30	Port Merch. Walls	Lisbon
		Came in for
	Mercurius, Waddle	Lisbon
	Pool ——	Arrived from
27	Watsons Adv. Watson	Lisbon
	Rainbow, Skold.	ditto
	Patience, Bowles	ditto
29	Betsy, Addis	Carolina
31	Agnes & Mary, Pottle	N.foundland
	Wm. & Thomas, Lander	London
	Cowes ——	Arrived from
29	Brunswick, Payne	Carolina
	Carter, Cork	Alderney
	Nicholas, Hains	Cherburgh
		Came in for
	St. Nicholas, Vessour	Callais
	Concordia, Trock	Hamburg
	Hellena, Guillaume	Carolina
	Dispatch, Wallace	Dublin
	Two Maries, Gordon	Southton
		Saild for
	Neptune, Stevens	Holland
	D. of Berwick, Basset	ditto
	London, Bourleigh	ditto
	Marygold, Joy	ditto
	Southampton ——	*arrived from*
30	Sarah, Withall	Oporto
	Expedition Packet	Guernsey
		Sailedfor
	Martlet, Martin	Amsterdam
	Portsmouth ——	Arrived from
		Came in for
30	Apollo, Brown	Jamaica

	Eagle, Stavely	Biddiford
	Mary & Ellen, Rush	Leverpool
	——, Slade	ditto
	Fidelia, Monkhouse	Dublin
	Mary-Ann, Craigh	Limerick
	——, Neman	Gottenburg
	Nancy, Tracy	Madeira
	Downs ——	Arrived from
30	K. of Portugal, Hughes	Lisbon
	Algarve, Olding	Faro
	St. John, Farrel	Antigua
31	Webster, Stevens	Chester
	Halsey & Suttle, Salisbury	ditto
1	Marys Reign, Jervoise	Barbadoes
	Wm. & Ann, Main	St. Kits
	Brittania, Farmer	New-York
		Remain for
	Two Dutch Ships	EastIndia
	A Dutch Ship	Guiney
	London, Pipon	Gibralter
	Concord, Spilman	Carolina
	Ann, Watson	Maryland
	Swallow, Hutchinson	Philadelphia
	Praleda, Herbert	Cork
	Minabilla, Blake	Lisbon
	Ann, Ebsworthy	Guiney
	Olliver, Pain	Gibralter
	Nassau, Spilman	Falmouth
	Hannah, Kilpatrick	Portsmouth
	Paradox, Righton	St. Kitts

Winds at **Deal.**

30 SW 31 W 1 NW

	Dublin ——	*arrived from*
	Providence, Steward	London
	Edw. & Mary, Littler	ditto
	Eagle,	ditto
	Cork ——	*Arrived from*
15	Martha, Purkess	Southton
	Jane & Betty, Jackson	Carolina
	William, Higat	Isle of Man
	Margaret, Robinson	Dublin
17	Hibernia, Comerford	Bristol
18	St. Louis, Evans	Bourdeaux
19	Richard, Crowley	Dublin
	Swift, Denroach	Bristol
20	Success, Allen	Ostend
	Mary, Phelan	Waterford
	Mary & Betty, M'Goran	Leverpool
	Success, Wadmore	Southton
21	Nestor, Moreshin	Hav
	Diligence, Milican	Isle of Man
	Henry, Richardson	Portsmouth
	Margaret, Bryon	Bruges
	Two Janes, Portivere	Dublin

12

Lloyd's List—the earliest surviving copy. 'Subscriptions are taken in at Three Shillings per quarter, at the Bar of Lloyd's coffee house in Lombard Street.' Exchange rates and market prices were on the first page, shipping movements on the second.

13

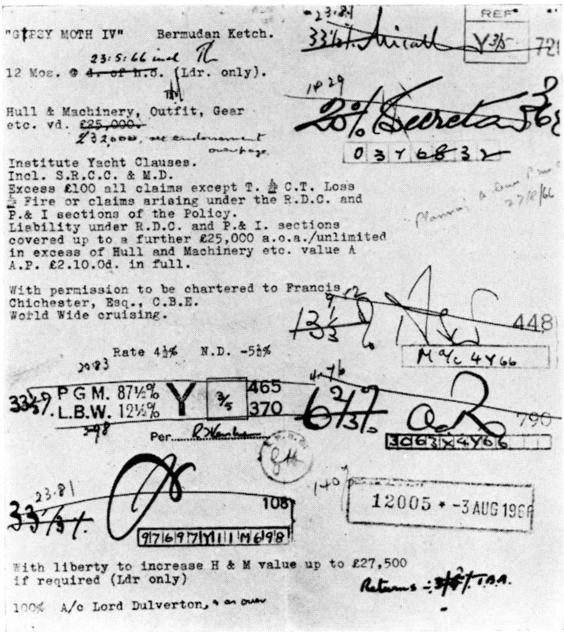

"GYPSY MOTH IV" Bermudan Ketch.

12 Mos. @ ~~4. of H.O.~~ (Ldr. only).

Hull & Machinery, Outfit, Gear
etc. vd. ~~£25,000.~~

Institute Yacht Clauses.
Incl. S.R.C.C. & M.D.
Excess £100 all claims except T. & C.T. Loss
& Fire or claims arising under the R.D.C. and
P.& I sections of the Policy.
Liability under R.D.C. and P.& I. sections
covered up to a further £25,000 a.o.a./unlimited
in excess of Hull and Machinery etc. value A
A.P. £2.10.0d. in full.

With permission to be chartered to Francis
Chichester, Esq., C.B.E.
World Wide cruising.

Rate 4½% N.D. -5½%

P G M. 87½%
L.B.W. 12½%
Y 3/5 465 370

Per.

12005 • -3 AUG 196

With liberty to increase H & M value up to £27,500
if required (Ldr only)

100% A/c Lord Dulverton,

Lloyd's not only insures transatlantic yachtsmen but through its Intelligence Department helps towards their safety. *Above*, the slip for *Gypsy Moth IV*. *Below, left*, Nicolette Milnes-Walker, lone Atlantic sailor, visits Lloyd's, and, *below, right*, aviator Sheila Scott is greeted by Paul Dixey, present Chairman of Lloyd's.

14

15

with those figures for the Chairman. All the same he thought I ought to have a word with his uncle, H. G. Chester, who had joined this syndicate more than sixty years ago, been Deputy Chairman of Lloyd's three times, and was now one of its elder statesmen. We crossed the corridor to one of the other offices where there were a couple of pleasant ladies sitting typing in a room lined with bookcases, containing huge and rather forbidding volumes with titles like Voyage Book and Loss Book, along with a set of reports of the Methodist Conference.

Henry Chester caught me looking at them and nodded. His uncle was still prominent in Methodism, he said. As for himself, he wasn't sure whether he'd say he was still a Methodist, but some of the principles had stuck. 'Not that you can have too many principles in this business, or you wouldn't make a profit. All the same, I've never written arms or ammunition.'

Most marine underwriters have pictures of ships on their walls; as a contrast to Henry Chester's oil rig, his uncle had the old *Mauretania* and the *Queen Mary*. Spry and lively looking at eighty-five, it hardly seemed possible that H. G. Chester had first sat at an underwriting box in 1903. In those days, he said, syndicates were much smaller—when he'd begun writing risks as a deputy in 1907, they'd had only ten names. In 1915 the firm had made him a member of Lloyd's. By then there were sixteen names. When he had taken over the syndicate in 1922, there had been seventeen.

Presently we moved on from the subject of the syndicate, and I asked him about the San Francisco earthquake, which was one of Lloyd's greatest catastrophes in this century. He hadn't lost much by it himself, he said, being in the marine market. What he did remember was the *Titanic*. In the outer office he still had the entry relating to her in the Loss Book, if I'd like to see it.

He pressed the buzzer and one of the secretaries came in. 'Which year was the *Titanic*?' he asked thoughtfully. '1912? April 14, wasn't it?'

He flicked the pages till he came to April 14. There were five sets of figures in the Loss column, written with a scratch pen in handwriting that had gone a gingery colour with time. 'That's my handwriting, sixty years ago. £542 on jewellery,' he read. '£5,000 on the hull to the brokers. Two additional lines to other brokers. We must have lost rather more than £8,000.'

Could he remember what it had been like in the Room when the news about the *Titanic* had come through? He thought for a moment, then admitted a trifle grudgingly that on that particular morning the market *had* been in a bit of a panic. 'After she was first notified as having hit the iceberg, the overdue brokers started rushing round.' Normally, he explained, the overdue brokers dealt in sailing ships that were held in the doldrums—if a ship became overdue, then the underwriters who had insured her would try to lay off a possible loss by reinsurance.

'Once the *Titanic* was known to have hit the iceberg, of course the rate was very high. There was one man who wrote a lot of reinsurance on her all the same—that was Sir Percy MacKinnon, who afterwards became Chairman of Lloyd's. I remember his father Benjamin,' added Mr Chester as an afterthought. 'He used to sit on the box wearing a top-hat. Anyway, Sir Percy MacKinnon believed the *Titanic* wouldn't sink, she was such a marvellous ship and there'd been so much publicity about her. So he wrote the reinsurance on her,' he repeated reflectively. 'He must have lost a lot of money.'

He put the Loss Books back, and the conversation darted about in the way that old men's conversation does. There'd been a ship called the *Pericles* he'd seen in London Docks, he remembered; he had been over her before her maiden voyage to Australia and she'd been a lovely ship. But she'd never got back from Australia. She'd gone down with a cargo of wool and there had been a big loss for the underwriters.

In those days of sail, he told me, the great worry was captains.

Nowadays his nephew had to worry about things like off-shore rigs and Greek ship-owners, but in those days what had mattered was whether the captain was any good. They'd kept a big book in the Room, where you could look up the record of any ship's master.

After that I thought we ought to be going, because his secretary had said Mr Chester might get tired if he talked too long, but he said talking about Lloyd's and ships never tired him. From his office window you could see Tower Bridge. Did I realize, he asked, that tucked away behind those skyscrapers was the original site of Edward Lloyd's coffee house?

For a moment I had a picture of the forest of masts that had once been there in the Pool of London, of seventeenth-century sea captains walking up greasy steps to the coffee house in Tower Street, and it occurred to me that at Lloyd's you never feel far from the sea. Other City offices sometimes seem to exist in a vacuum, a sort of artificial world of mining shares and cocoa futures without reference to the real one where people actually mine diamonds and plant cocoa.

At Lloyd's the ships are real, and it is part of the quality of the place.

What sort of people are Lloyd's names? Apart from having to have £75,000, Henry Chester told me, he didn't think there were many social trends you could read into it. On his own syndicate he had one peer, a theatrical impresario, one American, and a man who runs a firm that makes famous lorries. Most of the others were old employees, friends, brokers, people whom he'd simply come across in the way of business.

Later I had a look at Lloyd's members list where all the 7,000 names are listed. In the course of about a quarter of an hour's browsing, I came across about three minor members of the Royal Family, several judges and two cabinet ministers. (Membership of Lloyd's is, apart from farming, the only outside interest a Cabinet Minister does not have to give up on taking office.) Neither Edward Heath nor Harold Wilson are names at Lloyd's, but around fifty other MPs are. You might get a West Ham shirt if the syndicate that Jimmy Greaves is on were to go down: on the other hand there are no pop stars and not many actors. Stockbrokers are not allowed to become members of Lloyd's because they have liabilities of their own. Bookmakers or pools promotors might not get through, I was told, because there'd be some danger of their losing their money.

On one syndicate I counted the names of eight peers—but membership of Lloyd's is by no means an upper-class preserve. 'Even ten years ago,' I was told by an underwriter who serves on the Rota Committee, 'we'd have thought twice about someone who wasn't a gent. Nowadays that's all gone. You get some young chap who's built up a business from scratch, had it taken over and wants to make the money he's earned work for him. These are the sort of whizz-kids that Lloyd's today can do with.'

Is it possible, I asked the underwriter on the Rota Committee, for the occasional dodgy character to slip through the net? He said he didn't think so, because everyone who puts up for Lloyd's has to have a certificate showing that they have the funds they say they have. 'It's only possible if the chap issuing the certificate is bent, and normally we know these people. If you can't trust a chartered accountant, who do you trust?'

'I may be old-fashioned, but I like something with a bit of history about it.' Tradition, whether it is Lloyd's of London or the Elephant and Castle where he was brought up, is something that appeals to former heavyweight boxing champion Henry Cooper. When he comes down to Lloyd's he always takes a look at the famous treasure in the Nelson Room—just as when he goes back to the Elephant and Castle he deplores the sky-scrapers and impersonality. 'People have got better homes to live in but they've taken something away,' he says.

Not that it was simply his feeling for tradition that made Henry Cooper decide to invest his ring earnings in a syndicate at Lloyd's: having retired from the ring, he looks warily at the fate of other champions who didn't make the right sort of provision for the future. One man he knew, he said, had sunk £30,000 in a hotel project in Wales and lost the lot. Henry himself reckons he'd made a couple of hundred thousand when he left boxing, and he decided to put it in something where it could go on earning for him.

At the moment, he said, he had a good job in public relations. 'But there might come a time when my face had begun to fade a bit. That's when I'd be glad to have my money working for me.'

Henry Cooper is a name on two syndicates, writing both marine and non-marine business. His original contact with Lloyd's came through Harry Levene, the promoter, who always used to insure his fights at Lloyd's. One of the syndicate asked Henry if he'd ever thought of becoming a name; he went down to Lloyd's, had a look round, and decided to join Levene's friend's syndicate. He'd had to go through what seemed a mountain of bits of paper, four copies of everything, and was finally accepted as a name in 1971. He had spent about ten minutes in front of the Rota Committee, but it hadn't been very unnerving. 'Mostly,' he recalled with the air of a man to whom the question was predictable, 'they wanted to know about Cassius Clay.'

Did he worry about the idea of unlimited liability if anything went wrong? Henry Cooper said he supposed everybody must think about it sometimes, but as far as he was concerned he was with people he trusted. His underwriting agent had got his wife and his father both on the syndicate and Henry reckoned that was good enough for him. Only that week he had had a letter from the syndicate with a note of his first year's earnings and they looked pretty good—but what really mattered was trust.

'After all, they've been doing their underwriting three hundred years. They ought to know how to do it.'

At Lloyd's all underwriters are equal, but you are aware of a certain suspicion that marine underwriters are more equal than others. 'I suppose,' one broker said to me early on, 'this is going to be another bloody book about marine underwriting.'

In fact more than half the syndicates at Lloyd's are non-marine. To see what one of them was like, I sought out the current chairman of the Non-Marine Underwriters' Association, Mr Frank Barber. I would find him, I was told, at Box 309 in the gallery.

Mr Barber turned out to be a large, expansive, grey-haired man who was clearly regarded with considerable affection by the other people on his box. 'On this syndicate we're a mixture of blue blood and mongrels,' he said, and everyone roared with laughter.

I hadn't sat at a box where there hadn't been a pleasant atmosphere, but this one seemed pleasanter than most.

A young broker came in and asked if Mr Barber remembered writing a racing-car risk for somebody in Canada last year. Mr Barber said he might remember if he'd made any money on it.

The broker spread the slip on the table. It was in the name of a Canadian broker named Whitehead and seemed to be about eight racing cars in various formulas, without mentioning the names of the drivers.

I asked if it wasn't important to know the name of the person who was driving the racing car, and Mr Barber said no, not in this case; Whitehead was a firm they knew and trusted.

'If you were a racing driver in Canada, sir,' said the young broker, looking at me, 'you'd go to Whitehead.' The young broker seemed to be rather knowledgeable altogether about motor-racing. Eventually it turned out that he was a driver himself, and had driven a Formula II car in the Nuremberg 1,000-mile race last summer. Lloyd's had worked out a special insurance for racing drivers whose cars were being sponsored, and he'd sold quite a lot of policies while he was there.

I asked what the premium would be on a racing driver's life and he said that it might go up to 3 per cent. Mr Barber asked as a matter of interest what the rate for Indianapolis was and the broker said have a guess. Mr Barber said he guessed it would be around 10 per cent, and the broker said as a matter of fact, no, it was 12, sir.

'Coming back to this Whitehead cover,' Mr Barber enquired, 'what's a rolling chassis?'

'The car without the engine and the gearbox. The point is that half the value's in that—and in a modern car it won't smash under impact. It'll only go if the whole thing catches fire.'

Mr Barber took out his pen and the broker shut up. 'I think the thing is to write you a small line of, say, 2½ per cent,' declared Mr Barber courteously, 'and see how it goes.'

By this time it was about half-past four and the stream of brokers was drying up. Mr Barber suggested we might go up to his office and have a talk. On the oak door it simply said Frank Barber and Ors., meaning Others, which is the Lloyd's way of describing a syndicate.

Mr Barber explained that two-thirds of the syndicate is controlled by a firm called Wigham Richardson & Bevington. Mr Barber himself controls the other third, under the name Morgan, Fentiman & Barber. It had been Wigham Richardson & Bevington that had originally put up the money for him to become a Member. He had left school and gone to work in an accountant's office at £1 a week, then moved to Lloyd's in 1939, when he was sixteen.

On the syndicate he runs there are something like 120 names, each with a figure opposite them representing units of £5,000. The total of the figures was added up at the bottom of the list—it came to 690. 'That means 690 times £5,000.' He did the sort of rapid sum that Lloyd's men do on odd bits of paper. 'Three million four hundred and fifty thousand,' he said, making it sound like a lot of money. 'That's the amount of premium we can accept in a year.'

One of the differences from Chester's firm, he added, was that Wigham Richardson's were also brokers. Had I had explained to me the rather incestuous way in which brokers at Lloyd's could have an interest in underwriting syndicates as well? I said I'd heard of it, but it still seemed a bit hard to see how it worked out in practice. If an underwriter was in a sense the broker's employee, wouldn't the broker be able to lean on him sometimes to get better terms?

Mr Barber agreed that you might suppose it would be like that, but in practice it didn't happen. 'I can't recollect any occasion when I treated my own firm differently from any other. If anything they'll get a harder ride. That's why Lloyd's is Lloyd's. If I did let it make a difference I'd feel I'd let down all the other names on the syndicate. When one of the brokers becomes a name, I say, look you're not going to get any favours. But I still expect to see you and all your business. However I treat you,' he added, and laughed.

Because he himself came up the hard way, Frank Barber believes strongly in giving a helping hand to his staff. Four of the other people on his box are members of Lloyd's, made so by the firm. Most of them will soon have paid off out of profits. There are also three young men who he hopes will eventually come on the syndicate as well. 'I look forward to the day,' he said warmly, 'when they're all on.'

In the twelve years that he has been senior underwriter on the syndicate, Frank Barber has never had to ask any of his names to pay up on a year's dealings. Although he said underwriters were reluctant to talk about profits, he agreed that even in the lean years of the mid-1960s the syndicate had managed to keep in the black.

What did Mr Barber see as the real skill of underwriting? He said it was three things—attracting brokers to his box, not being afraid to write a big commitment on the good business and turning down the bad. 'When you look at it, Unlimited Liability's a marvellous principle,' he said. 'It's like what Dr Johnson said about the man being hanged. It concentrates the mind.'

After a bit he suggested I might meet the other two underwriters on the syndicate and we went into a small office adjoining Mr Barber's. Both rooms are simply used as extra accommodation to the box if the underwriters need somewhere to write something in peace or have a meeting with a broker. There are no secretaries, no impedimenta—all the business of corresponding with names is done from Wigham Richardson's main office. 'If you open that cupboard you won't find any gin in it,' said Mr Barber. 'It's all files.'

Sitting in the other room there were two underwriters, Jack Beecham and Charles Flaxman. Mr Barber looked at them benignly, as if they were a couple of prodigies of whom he was rather proud.

'They're the intellectuals, the ones who get *The Times* crossword done before ten o'clock.'

Beecham, a short dark man with glasses, grinned and said what did he mean, he'd done it before he got to the office. Charles Flaxman was the tall, rather melancholy-looking one. Later he said he had to get home to Southend because his local amateur dramatic company was rehearsing *Twelfth Night*. I didn't like to actually ask if he was playing Aguecheek because I thought it would be type-casting, but it turned out that he was.

Since they'd been introduced as the intellectuals, I asked if they read a lot. Charles Flaxman said he read everything from novels to sauce-bottle labels. Jack Beecham read a lot anyway because he specialized in libel.

I thought that sounded interesting and he said it was. So were amusement parks, which was the other thing he wrote. Not that he actually liked amusement parks—he'd seen Coney Island once but hadn't taken much notice. 'I stay away from them,' he said. 'You can't write that sort of business if you see what happens.'

I asked if that meant the amusement parks were a fairly uncertain risk, and he said they certainly were. 'You can get some degree of inspection, and in the US they've got some codes of safety. But it's a very hazardous business.' The syndicate had had a couple of major losses in California in 1956, when a lot of people fell off the big skywheel—it had cost the underwriters about $200,000. The other thing was that it was often practically impossible to tell if someone was making a truthful claim or not. 'You get some people who'll pretend there was something faulty with the machinery. They've only got to step off a roundabout backwards and it's worth $200 to them.'

I asked if they included circuses with amusement parks and Jack Beecham looked cautious.

'We used to write circuses but we don't now,' he said. 'Not since we had a circus where an elephant lifted its picket stake, which is the thing it's tied to when the circus isn't working. Well, this elephant wandered round the town, just for a walk, I suppose, and it came to an open lot where there was a truck parked. It started scratching its bottom on the side of the truck, and it was still doing it when the driver came back. I suppose he'd been drinking in some bar, and he didn't believe it when he saw the elephant. So he started belting it, and I'm afraid the elephant sat on him. That cost us $43,000.'

I wondered how the syndicate came to write these rather unusual risks, amusement parks and libels. Jack Beecham explained that the syndicate had started in 1928, and the underwriter in those days had been a man with a typically Lloyd's feeling for innovation. The tradition had grown up that the syndicate was ready to look at any unusual class of business, and the tradition had stuck.

From the amusement parks we moved on to libel. Jack Beecham said that about twenty television interviewers and journalists have libel insurance with Lloyd's; in the case of one well-known anchorman on their books, the cover would be about £15,000 for a premium of around £50. Most novelists don't insure, but 60 per cent of the best-known publishers do.

Mr Beecham added that most provincial newspapers insure,

but London ones don't—in the case of a mass circulation paper, he thought, the premium would be so big, it wouldn't be worth it. Once, one of the weeklies had had a policy with the syndicate, and there had very nearly been a big claim when a reviewer had written about a book by Lord Beaverbrook. The reviewer had implied that Beaverbrook tended to put a rather good complexion on his own part in recent history, and Beaverbrook had issued a writ.

The upshot had been that Jack Beecham had spent a whole day rushing round in taxis getting hold of solicitors, brokers and various editorial people. At last he had returned home, pretty well exhausted, and turned on the radio to hear the news that Lord Beaverbrook had died suddenly.

'It was,' he said, 'just about the most dramatic end to a libel case you could imagine.'

One of Beecham's first risks as a libel underwriter was over Laurie Lee's modern classic, *Cider with Rosie*. 'It was a dream of a book, but unfortunately he'd put in a bit about how when they were children in the Cotswolds they used to go up the hill to watch a local factory catching fire. In the book he said something about the fire being an annual event to swell their profits. It so happened there was only one such factory in Stroud, and they sued him. He'd just won the *Evening Standard* prize of £1,000 for the book, and under the usual author's indemnity to the publisher, he had to pay up. I'm afraid it cost him nearly all the prize money.'

I asked what other sort of specialist writers they insured; along the office bookshelf I had noticed about eight editions of a restaurant guide by one of Britain's foremost specialists in *haute cuisine*. Jack Beecham said they'd insured this writer since he'd brought out his first book, because there were a lot of ways you could inadvertently go wrong in the food-guide business.

'Our contribution to better eating in the United Kingdom,' said Mr Barber, and everyone laughed again. By now it was time for him to go, and Mr Flaxman to be off to his *Twelfth*

Night rehearsal. I asked Jack Beecham what he was going to do, and he said he was going home to have a read.

'*Tom Brown's Schooldays*,' he said. 'It's my favourite book, I've read it ten times already. What's more, there's no risk of libel.'

PART TWO

The Modern Market

4
America Discovers Lloyd's

It often happens that a great innovator's chance comes at a time of crisis. It may be an art-form grown threadbare, an administration grown corrupt—it is the need for reform that makes the individual's opportunity. Lloyd's, in its nature, has always been a place for pioneers. Just as Angerstein had cleaned up the gambling market of the 1760s, so the opportunity came, over a century later, for the man who was to be the founder of the modern Lloyd's.

Perhaps it is not quite true to say that Lloyd's in the 1880s was in a state of crisis, but it was certainly in a period of downswing. Business had begun to drift away to the big marine insurance companies. Lloyd's might still be a unique institution, but it was in danger of losing out to more outward-looking rivals.

Partly, perhaps, it had been a gentlemen's occupation for too long. When one outstanding underwriter, F. W. Marten, moved into an expanding world market by writing enormous lines on his marine risks, the Room shook its collective head in horror. As far as non-marine business went, there were a few boxes where you could insure against fire risks, but that was all. Lloyd's, it seemed possible, could decay into a venerable institution inhabited by elderly gentlemen with distant memories of tea-clippers.

Such was Lloyd's when there arrived, in 1880, a shrewd, rather dapper-looking young man named Cuthbert Heath. The son of an admiral, he had been turned down for the navy. Possibly a psychoanalyst could make something of the fact. The essence of his contribution was that he steered Lloyd's away from what had been, till now, an almost total interest in marine matters.

Heath became an underwriting member in 1883, and almost immediately began writing what seemed to the market novel, if eccentric, business. Fire policies had existed before, but Heath invented a new sort which not merely covered a company against fire, but against the loss of business that followed. He wrote reinsurance for a company called the Hand-in-Hand, in which his father had an interest.

The more conservative-minded figures in the Captains' Room may have deplored such ideas, but there was nothing in Lloyd's rules to stop Heath's innovations. Soon afterwards he was asked if he would write the reinsurance for the American branch of another English company, and he did so. It was a landmark in the history of Lloyd's—the first American risk ever written in the non-marine market.

In 1887, Heath moved into another field which seemed startlingly new. In those days there was no such thing as an insurance against being burgled. One day a broker was insuring his own furniture against fire with Heath, and asked him, since the crime-rate was on the increase, if he'd mind insuring him against burglary too? Almost as a joke, Heath wrote it. Within two years the broker's firm was advertising that it could effect insurance at Lloyd's against theft and robbery, with or without violence.

Other innovations followed. One day a relative of Heath's lost a piece of jewellery which she had insured with him against theft. There was no cover for loss, he explained, but immediately saw a new opportunity—if you could insure against burglary, why not against losing your jewels as well? He went back to his box, thought the matter over, and came up with a premium-rate of ten shillings for each £100 of cover. It was not only the first form of insurance against loss, but the premium-rate stood for fifty years. Almost as a natural follow-up came the idea of insuring diamonds in transit.

Within a few years of Heath's arrival at Lloyd's the market was insuring things which, in the 1870s, would have been unheard of. They were insuring factories in Chicago and Baltimore against fire, they were insuring farmers in Southern Europe against hail damage. In 1901 came Lloyd's first motor insurance—even though it was written in the marine market, and the car was treated as a ship navigating on dry land. By the time Lloyd's wrote the first aviation policy in 1911 they had at least moved a little away from the marine image—the pilot was referred to as 'the driver'.

In all these new departures the prime mover had been Cuthbert Heath. 'His name is honoured today,' writes Gibb, 'not because he started non-marine underwriting at Lloyd's but because he revolutionised, both at Lloyd's and elsewhere, the business of non-marine insurance and enormously widened the service he offered to the commercial world . . . Today whenever a man says that Lloyd's will insure anything, he is paying an . . . unconscious tribute to the genius of Cuthbert Heath.'

In the story of the modern Lloyd's two things stand out. One was Heath's invention of a non-marine market. The other was America's discovery of Lloyd's. The two events were not linked in the sense that one caused the other, but they were linked just the same. The point was that Lloyd's was doing the right thing at the right moment for the huge and expanding American market.

In the past there had been many links with America. Lloyd's agents had been appointed there since the beginning of the nineteenth century, and in 1840 a chairman of Lloyd's had made a six months' tour of the United States, the first ever by a chairman in office to a foreign country.

Even so the links had been formal ones, such as there might have been with any other trading country. (If you look at the index of Frederick Martin's *History of Lloyd's*, published in 1876, it is significant that you will find America mentioned only twice, and non-marine insurance not at all.)

But now, as the 1890s began, something completely different happened, and on a completely different scale. With her new and booming industries, America was of necessity insurance-minded. A new breed of capitalist was growing up, many of them immigrants who had started from nothing and had no resources to fall back on. Soon they were asking for more insurance than the home-grown industry could cope with. They began to look abroad to Europe, and they found Lloyd's. Of all the European insurers, nothing else quite matched their own individualistic spirit.

What is important to notice, looking back, is that none of this could have happened without the newly-created non-marine market. The great commercial need of the booming America of the 1890s was cover for its new-found prosperity. If a Boston millionaire wanted insurance for anything from his factory to his mistress's jewels, he could get it at Lloyd's. An Illinois saloon-keeper could get cover at Lloyd's – and nowhere else – to protect him from the new law which said he was responsible for damage done by anyone who had got drunk in his saloon. The first American motor policy came in 1907, for $2,500 on the White steam car in Chicago. Across the whole booming, rip-roaring continent a new name was beginning to be known—the name of Lloyd's of London.

Indeed, it was becoming so well known that it was being borrowed. In 1910 there were 37 different insurance companies in New York alone, all trading, prosperously but unofficially, under the name of Lloyd's.*

Ultimately the test of an insurer is whether he pays up, and in 1906 the non-marine market faced its biggest test—the San Francisco earthquake. In the space of a single minute, 30,000

* In American insurance jargon the name has come to be almost an adjective: in the State of New York, for instance, a successful 'Lloyd's syndicate' is still thriving. It writes business for about 10 names, operates on a modest scale on the same pattern, but has no connection whatever with the original.

houses were destroyed, including nearly 500 city blocks. Seven hundred people were dead and over a quarter of a million homeless. In the insurance world the reverberations continued for months. If a building was covered for fire, some of the companies claimed, then the policy would not apply if the fire had been caused or preceded by an earthquake.

'More than a third of the San Francisco fire business,' wrote *The Times* in a cautious leader, 'is estimated to be in the hands of British offices, where the calculation of liability must be a matter of some anxiety.' On another page the paper's Berlin correspondent wrote that among the German companies, where many of the San Francisco risks had been insured, 'the view is expressed that where a building collapsed and then took fire, the insurance companies are not liable'.

In the event many, though not the British, companies did repudiate their liability. Lloyd's did not. The final claim on their underwriters was in the region of $100,000,000—a staggering figure for those days. It was, one might say, the moment of truth. Lloyd's had not merely survived it, but created a new and massive goodwill for the future.

From now on it would no longer be a market which primarily insured ships. Nor would its business be primarily British. The stress would be increasingly American, and increasingly on the non-marine side.

Today just on half of all Lloyd's business comes from the United States. How, when all countries operate laws to protect their domestic markets, does this work out in practice? In the United States insurers work under licence—in most towns you will find the agent, or representative, of the main insurance companies. 'If you want to place an insurance,' says Keith Brown, partner in Lloyd's American attorneys, 'you go to an agent who is licensed under state law. In the early days the licensing authorities didn't know what to make of Lloyd's. It wasn't chauvinism—they were simply suspicious of the idea of a risk being placed with some distant insurer who wasn't subject to the local laws.'

Since then, insurance regulations have been adapted to admit Lloyd's. In two states, Illinois and Kentucky, Lloyd's is freely licensed. In other states, an agent may place insurance with Lloyd's only when he has exercised what the law calls 'due diligence' in trying to place the risk in the domestic market. The point is that when he *has* exercised due diligence he can go to Lloyd's—which in its nature and with its resources writes many kinds of insurance that the domestic companies do not. Again, the scale of a risk may often be so large that it cannot all be covered in the local market. In this case, too, the business is likely to come to Lloyd's.

Meanwhile what about the regulations in the two states where Lloyd's are licensed—Kentucky and, more significantly because of its huge industrial importance, Illinois? Here insurance can be placed direct: in Chicago it will go through the offices of Lord, Bissell and Brook, attorneys-at-law. Roughly having the same function as Lloyd's Policy Signing Office, the attorneys' role is to see that both state laws and Lloyd's own rules are complied with. 'The sort of thing we might get,' says John Smith, the attorney who looks after Lloyd's Illinois business, 'is a broker coming up with a tailored policy that turns out to be thinly veiled strike insurance. I'll have a look at it and it might raise questions in my mind as to whether it was against public policy, as laid down by the Illinois code, which says that an employer can't insure against his employees going on strike.' To take another example, the policy might be for financial guarantee insurance, which is permitted by the Illinois code but not at Lloyd's. In this case John Smith might also query, and if necessary, stop it.

Probably the most impressive symbol of Lloyd's trans-Atlantic link is the American Trust Fund. This had its origins in 1939, when American brokers became concerned as to what might happen to their claims on London underwriters if war broke out. Before 1939 it had been a common practice for underwriters to leave their premiums in the United States untouched. Since Britain had gone off the Gold Standard in 1931, it reduced exchange problems and gave confidence to American brokers.

Now, however, the situation was different. No American broker supposed that a Lloyd's underwriter would default; nor, says Keith Brown, did they greatly fear the possibility that Britain would be overrun by the Nazis. 'What they did fear was that the British Government would impose restrictions on the international transfer of currencies. If that did happen, what were the chances of American claims being met?'

There was only one possible answer, and it was both bold and far-reaching—that all American premiums should be paid into a separate account, to be held in the United States. Underwriters would receive their profits only after claims, or the possibility of claims, had been allowed for. The machinery was rapidly set up and in August 1939 the American Trust Fund opened with capital resources of $40 million. Today it stands at more than $1240 million.

Meanwhile, how does the business actually come to Lloyd's? Against the background of the American link, it is time to look at the other person involved in any underwriting deal—the Lloyd's broker.

5
The Brokers' Men

One of the astonishing things about the City of London is the number of large and prosperous firms you have never heard of. In ten minutes' walk around Leadenhall Street you will see so many merchant banks, investment companies and discount houses that you wonder how they all make a living.

Among those who make their bread and butter with jam are the insurance brokers. Around 260 of them are accredited to Lloyd's, which entitles them to put 'and at Lloyd's' on their notepaper as if it was their country seat.

At the top of the pyramid are the seven known, with respectful envy, as the 'broker barons'. These are the firms of Bland, Welch; C. T. Bowring; Hogg Robinson and Gardner Mountain; Leslie and Godwin; J. H. Minet; Sedgwick Forbes; and Willis, Faber and Dumas.

Today such firms are among the biggest invisible exporters in the City. Most are old established—Sedgwick Forbes, for instance, is the result of a recent merger of two of the biggest firms, Sedgwick Collins and Price Forbes, both of which started back in the golden age of insurance in the mid-nineteenth century. Broking firms tend to get taken over or merged so often you get an almost kaleidoscopic effect. In the brief time I was busy at Lloyd's there were at least three large-scale mergers.

Bowrings began even earlier, in 1811, when Benjamin Bowring, a clock-maker from Exeter, set off for Newfoundland and founded a trading company. Today his commercial progeny includes fifty-four companies, ranging from insurance broking to fish oils and a merchant bank. The Bowring empire operates from its own skyscraper near the Tower of London and ranks as the sixth largest exporter in Britain. Its shares are quoted not only on the Stock Exchange but on the stock markets of most Common Market countries too.

Most brokers have a series of allied or controlled companies so that a chart of them looks like a pedigree of the House of Hanover. Sedgwick Forbes, for instance, has recently opened offices in five Common Market capitals. Willis Faber owns sixteen companies abroad, right down to one in Mexico called Willis Faber y Wigg. To complicate things still further, most of the larger brokers also run several syndicates at Lloyd's. It may look to the outsider like a good example of having your cake and eating it, but Lloyd's insists that it works.

Nearly two-thirds of the risks placed by Lloyd's brokers are from the United States; all the main offices have links with companies in the major American cities, who are known variously as correspondents or producers. If a hotel group or an airline wants to insure, they will probably go direct to one of the big brokers in New York or Chicago. Small-town brokers will pass some risks to what are known as the surplus-line brokers, who deal in the kind of specialized insurance for which they will look to Lloyd's.

Thus the risks which arrive in the Room via the brokers' offices may have started anywhere from Seattle to Canyon City. 'In London,' said one Chicago broker, 'if you ask people the way to Lloyd's they're quite capable of directing you to the bank. At home you mention Lloyd's of London, and everyone's heard of it.'

At the heart of this reputation is Lloyd's willingness to take risks that no one else will look at. One broker told me that among the more precarious insurances he had placed was one for stock-car racing in Ohio. 'I was stopping in a small town when this guy came up and said he'd heard I was from Lloyd's. He promoted stock-car racing and wondered if I could get him some liability insurance to cover accidents to spectators. I shuddered. They'd got thousands of country people on a day out, and the only protection was a few barrels. Most of the cars were home-made and they had these bloody great engines, aero engines mostly. I think we were crazy, but we placed it at $500 premium a meeting—that was fifteen years ago. It'd be around $10,000 now. We had claims all right—wheels disappearing into the crowd, felling little Freddy. All the same I don't think anyone got killed.'

What does an insurance broker actually do? Historically the verb 'to broke' has the same origin as 'to broach'. A broker, says the Oxford Dictionary, is 'one who acts as a middle-man in bargains'. At Lloyd's people talk about 'broking' somebody in the sense of selling them something.

If you want to insure your house or your car, you may quite possibly go to an insurance company direct. If the risk is a little more complicated or specialized, you will need to go to a broker. He will then shop around the various companies and try to get you the best terms, taking his own commission.

If on the other hand your risk is something like an oil rig or a petro-chemical plant, then the chances are that you will need one of the 258 brokers accredited to Lloyd's, whose representatives are the only people allowed to do business in the Room. Each day around 3,000 of their brokers circulate in it, and could be said to be its life-blood. Underwriters occasionally say hard things of brokers, but cannot do without them—if no brokers come to an underwriter's box, he does no business. Basically, the relationship remains good, if only because it has to. 'Broker and underwriter stay on good terms,' said one broker, 'because we both want to be in business tomorrow.'

In essence the code which governs dealing between the two is simple. If the underwriter asks the broker something that is not on the slip and he knows the answer, he is bound to give it. If the broker has information which could materially affect the risk but fails to give it, it is called a 'pick-up'. In practice this almost never happens, if only because a broker who did pick an underwriter up would soon get known in the market.

I asked one leading marine underwriter how often he had been picked up in his time at Lloyd's, and he said only once that he could swear to, but probably a few other times when he suspected it but couldn't prove it. 'I'd say there were three kinds of brokers in the Room,' he told me. 'There are those who wouldn't let me write a risk if they thought there was anything wrong with it. There are the great majority who are perfectly trustworthy, but you've got to read the slip. Finally, and very rarely, there are a few who'd deliberately try to mislead you.'

Brokers come in all shapes and sizes. There are experts who specialize in anything from oceanology to bloodstock. There are long-haired young brokers who get decanted from vans, a bit like police at a demonstration, at ten o'clock every morning outside the Room. There are cheerful middle-aged men in pinstripes who tend to call the underwriters 'Sir'. (Though this is not invariably a mark of respect. One broker told me he might call an underwriter 'sir' if he thought he wasn't being helpful.)

All insurance men have to be optimists but with the brokers it physically shows, a sort of enthusiastic glow like a comedian's smile for his entrance. 'The moment a broker goes into the Room,' said one, 'it's got to be the finest risk he's ever seen. Even when he's been turned down on some terrible risk the good broker will go round looking puzzled, wondering why the hell he couldn't place it. In the last analysis you broke yourself. That's the real secret.'

Almost as much built in as the broker's optimism is a sort of hectic energy. A lot of brokers give the impression of visibly burning themselves up, which may be worth it, when you consider that a top broker can easily earn upwards of £50,000. A director of one firm told me he'd be away on Thursday, he had to go to a two-hour meeting in Los Angeles: he thought he might drop in to see a couple of people in New York on the way back, but hoped to be home by Sunday. I asked another broker what he did at weekends. 'Walk,' he said, making it sound like the training for a marathon of some sort. 'My wife and I walk along the beach at Bexhill. We're always walking. We must walk for bloody miles.'

At first sight you would hardly take Mr Peter Wright for a broker. Sitting in his office overlooking the Pool of London, he has the greying, serious look of a kindly country doctor. It is only when he starts to talk that you sense a bubbling, volcanic energy: Mr Wright has the sort of conversational *panache* which marks the true broker. He first came to Lloyd's in the mid-1940s, and you feel he has loved every minute since. 'Once they let me out into the market,' he says, 'I knew it was my world. I handled it my way. I realized it was all a matter of personal relationships and it still is. How else do you persuade an underwriter to give you a reasonable rate on fresh eggs in paper bags from Montevideo to Liverpool?'

Today, as a director of the giant broking firm of Sedgwick Forbes, he finds himself having to sit behind an office desk a good deal more than he would choose to. When he is not at his desk, or travelling between San Francisco or Melbourne and London, he lives with his family in a country house at Cowden in Kent, where with typical broker's energy he spends his weekends shovelling earth or blasting out music on a hi-fi. 'I like Range Rovers and Beethoven and machines,' he says happily. 'I'll have to go on doing something when I retire, so I've built myself a workshop.'

Meanwhile, despite the office desk, he said, there was the compensation of being right in on so many new developments. One of the risks he was working on now was for a new oil rig off the coast of Cromarty.

'This is the biggest damn platform ever built,' he said with a mixture of awe and exuberance. 'We're going to have to persuade underwriters to give us cover for £40 million.'

Another risk Sedgwick's were handling was for the biggest liquid natural gas carrier-ship ever built. She would carry 125,000 cubic metres of natural gas and be worth nearly £30 million. 'Underwriters are going to have a lot of worries over that. Our job's to put their fears to bed. A broker's got to be a psychologist and a salesman put together.'

How far, I asked him, would a broker actually go to get the best terms for a customer wanting insurance—was it a bit like a barrister trying to make out the best possible case for his client?

Mr Wright looked thoughtful, and replied that he didn't think it was quite the same. 'A barrister hopes not to see his client a second time. I want to go on doing business with mine and what's more important I've got to go on doing business with the underwriter.' There were brokers, he said, who would try to get the rates down so far that they practically ruined the market. 'When they drive too hard a bargain it doesn't help anyone. If things go wrong, they'll just have a tougher job to place the business next year.'

I asked him if he would always tell the underwriter all the facts about a risk and he said he would, except that like any salesman the broker's job was to put the facts in the best light. 'The bottle is always half full, never half empty. I don't have to put ideas into his head. If I'm placing a drilling-barge in the Gulf of Mexico, I wouldn't think it necessary to tell an underwriter that they get hurricanes there. Or, for that matter, that earthquakes happen in California or that the Baltic ices up. I don't have to tell him things he's deemed to know in the normal course of business.'

What about the way he actually approaches an underwriter? Mr Wright said disarmingly that he tended to talk too much. Theoretically it was supposed to be a bad thing to over-broke, but he was such a talker that he went on even after the underwriter had picked up his pen. 'I think they write things just to get rid of me.' All the same, he said more seriously, you could never forget that the relationship with the underwriter mattered. He himself had just served four years on the Committee of Lloyd's, and his loyalty was to Lloyd's as well as Sedgwick's.

Having said which, there were obviously different ways in which you might approach an underwriter, or which broker you might send to him. 'I can think of one underwriter who's a Rotarian. If we had an awkward risk to show him we might send a broker who was another Rotarian. A few years ago we had a broker who was rather theatrical, a bit camp. We'd often send him with a difficult risk because he'd have them all rolling with laughter on the box and they'd write it.'

I asked if it wasn't a good thing to approach an underwriter when he'd lunched well, and Mr Wright grinned. 'Before we moved to Lime Street the old Room was very warm. There were chaps who would tend to doze after lunch, and we came out of the cool into the warm Room, sharp as tacks. Now we've got the new Room and it's air-conditioned, so it's the other way round. We're the ones at a disadvantage.'

Even so, he said, there were underwriters who liked a good lunch and didn't want to think too hard in the afternoon. If you wanted to persuade them to write something they weren't too keen on, then the afternoon might be the right time to raise it. 'The point is you've got to know your man. That doesn't mean being smart or aggressive—it's part of your stock-in-trade.'

A few years back, Mr Wright said, Sedgwick's had placed a huge construction insurance on the Mangla Dam in Pakistan. 'There are a lot of underwriters who wouldn't write a dam-under-construction if you paid them a hundred per cent. We had to have cover for $75 million.' The brokers had spent a lot of time planning the marketing of the risk—breaking it up into layers, which were in turn backed by reinsurance.

'In effect,' explained Mr Wright, 'we were creating a kind of jigsaw puzzle. When it was pieced together it formed the complete cover the client wanted. Each piece was so designed as to make it attractive to a particular section of the market, and even the most anti-dams-under-construction underwriters found it difficult not to write the risk the way we planned it. We got one lot of underwriters to cover the $75 million policy, and another lot of underwriters to reinsure them. And because we put in a huge deductible, it meant that the reinsuring underwriters weren't going to have to bear the first $30 million worth of claims. With a premium of $250,000 staring him in the face, it was practically impossible for any underwriter to refuse it.'

Even so, Peter Wright recalls, it took some broking. 'I used to go to one underwriter's box and broke it to him for about half an hour. Then I'd come away exhausted, so drained that I had to get out of the Room and go for a walk by the river before I tackled the next underwriter.'

How competitive, I asked, was the world of the broker? A few days before, I had gone round with a young aviation broker who had suddenly dashed across the Room after another broker. The point was that he had seen him going to a box where he himself had already discussed a particular risk. We arrived just as the other broker was showing the underwriter the slip.

'I rather think we're on the same business.' The broker I was with looked mildly indignant, the underwriter looked mildly amused, the other broker looked mildly crestfallen.

'I don't think there's much I can do.' The underwriter gave the other man a tolerant nod. 'My rule is to favour the holding broker.' The other man went off, still looking crestfallen, and the broker I was with wished him better luck next time. He didn't seem ironic, simply friendly.

I told Mr Wright this story and he laughed and said this sort of thing went on in the market all the time. It was all part of trying to get the best terms for your client, and any broker in the market had to be constantly looking over his shoulder to see what the opposition were up to. Meanwhile, in the case of a very big risk, a client might ask several firms to produce a report. 'Say for example somebody got the go-ahead for the

Channel Tunnel. They'd probably put the insurance out to tender among half a dozen brokers, and we'd all put it together in various ways, with different rates, higher or lower deductibles and so on. Even so, the successful firm would probably be the one that had the best working relations with underwriters.'

One of the brokers' most important roles in the market is to innovate new kinds of insurance. At Sedgwick Forbes the tradition of pioneering is a long one, including the construction risk on the Boulder Dam, the insurance of the Dionne quintuplets, and the first Film Producer's Indemnity, which nowadays all producers take out to cover the possibility of their not completing a film because, for example, of the star's illness.

I asked Mr Alan Parry, a non-marine broker at Sedgwick's, for an example of the sort of innovating risks the firm were engaged on now. He said one of the largest was for an American plant using a new method of making synthetic natural gas – even though it might sound like a contradiction in terms – from a mixture of methane, coal and shale. The plant was going to cost $27 million and the process was entirely new. A pilot scheme had worked in Europe, but nobody had ever tried to make it on this scale. 'What they really need is an insurance that the thing works at all,' says Mr Parry. 'It's a bit like saying, because a light aircraft works, so will the Concorde.'

How long, I asked, might it take to prepare an insurance on something as complex and difficult as this? Mr Parry said it might often take months or more, but in this particular case Sedgwick's had worked extremely fast. It had only been three weeks since they had had the original enquiry from the American brokers; since then they had begun to evaluate the risk and brought in their own oil and petro-chemical experts. Within another month, he hoped, they would be able to start approaching underwriters with the information.

Such detailed planning does not only happen on very large risks. Mr Parry introduced me to one of his staff, Bill Williams, who specializes in Medical Malpractice, the type of insurance which medical associations take out to cover possible mistakes by their members. 'You could say it's to insure a doctor against the possibility of his taking out someone's liver when they've really come in to have their big toe straightened,' explained Mr Williams. Only about twelve underwriters at Lloyd's write Medical Malpractice; even so it brings in $5 million premium income a year. When he goes to see underwriters, Mr Williams can give them complete records of premiums and claims right down to the fact that in 1971 $110,000 was paid out for claims against surgeons in Colorado, while Arkansas dentists cost underwriters nothing. 'If I can produce figures like that,' said Mr Williams, 'it helps to sell the insurance, because underwriters can see which categories are likely to produce claims.'

About half the people you see in the Room are young, long-haired, and with the slightly hungry look that seems to go with broking. When a young broker starts he is likely to work first as an initialling or 'scratch' boy, simply going round the Room getting underwriters to initial a risk already verbally agreed to.

From this he will graduate to actual broking. 'There's nowhere else,' Mr Alan Parry told me, 'where if you're good, you can go up so quickly.' One of the things Mr Parry remembers from his own early days in the Room was how helpful underwriters had been to him. 'They'll always take time,' he said, 'to help you understand the business. It's like a university in that way.'

Typical of the young brokers of Lloyd's today is Michael White. The day I went round the Room with him it happened to be his twenty-sixth birthday. A cheerful, fresh-faced young man, he has been a marine broker with Sedgwick Forbes for five years. He earns rather more than £2,500 a year and lives at Upminster with his wife and two children. Originally, he said, he had come from Stepney, where his father is a lorry driver. 'He often used to drive past Lloyd's on his way through the City from Aldgate,' Michael said. 'I remember him saying to my brother and me, it'd be a good place to work.' Whether it had been as a result of this he wasn't quite sure, but his elder brother had gone into insurance, and Michael himself had started work as a clerk in Sedgwick's Policy Department at sixteen. After three years he had begun to find it boring. He had just started thinking of looking around for something else when he had been sent for and asked if he'd like to work in the Room.

'The first time I went in,' he told me, 'I thought I'd never learn the geography. In fact it took me about a year to get to know all the boxes.' The other thing that had slightly bothered him was whether he ought to try to put on an accent. 'Then one day an underwriter said, "Thank goodness for someone who's being himself. Don't change it." ' The words had meant a lot to Michael, and today he considers his East End background if anything as an advantage: people from the working class, he said, tended to have more ambition.

I quoted to him what the marine underwriter had said about there being three kinds of brokers, and asked him which sort he thought he belonged to. Michael laughed and said he hoped the first—if Sedgwick's sent a broker into the Room he went with their reputation, and that was something a young broker was taught from the beginning. The skill in approaching an underwriter lay in judging his mood, not from the point of view of trying to put one over on him, but knowing how his mood might vary.

'You can go to an underwriter one day, he'll argue and he won't write it. But you don't give up at the first attempt. It often happens that I'll get thrown out one day, then go in next day and get it done.' There was, he said, an enormous variation—you got days when everything went right, and others where nothing did. His wife would always know the moment he came home whether he'd had a good day or a bad one.

The essence of the broker's job is independence. For two or three hours each day Michael will discuss the day's business with other brokers or the head of his department—all the rest of his time is spent in the Room. At nine-thirty each morning there is a meeting in Sedgwick's office to look at the morning's cables, a lot of which will have come from their American producers. With the Assistant Director, Michael will discuss his own particular risks and how they should be presented. Then he goes to the Room, stays there till five, then back to the office until six-thirty.

What particular risk, I asked, was he hoping to place today? Michael said that this morning they had had a telex from an American producer. It was a relatively small risk, but for an oil company who were important clients. He wanted to get most of it written by this evening, but not all. It didn't do for the producers over there to think that things were too easy, he said, because often they weren't. The risk itself was for something called Cost of Control for a drilling-rig in the North Sea. It was a bit complicated, he said, but he'd try to explain it simply.

'If an oil company drills a well and they hit a gas pocket, there can be an explosion, which can lead to pollution. Sometimes you might be able to plug the hole with drilling-mud. On the other hand if there's a high pressure, they'd need to drill a relief well, which could be very expensive.'

I thought this seemed fairly straightforward, and Michael said that the complicated part lay in the way the insurance had been arranged. Had I had explained to me the way in which a lot of world-wide companies nowadays insured themselves? Because they were so big, it was cheaper for them to form what was called a captive, an insurance company of their own. This would stand their smaller claims. To cover the really big ones, the captive company would reinsure, very often at Lloyd's.

In this particular drilling operation, he said, there were several oil companies involved. The largest one had now gone self-insured in the way he had described. But the other companies – known as the co-venturers – still needed an insurance. The American broker had arranged it on a basis of all the co-venturers paying their share of the premium, with a minimum deposit of $14,000. 'What he'd overlooked was that this particular client only had four and a half per cent of the whole enterprise. The client had understood that his minimum deposit would be only $2,500, which is reasonable according to his proportion.'

Now Michael's job was to go round the Room, explain to the underwriters that there had been a human error by the US broker, and ask them if they'd agree that this particular client's deposit could be reduced. He had already got the leading underwriter to agree, but some of the others might take a bit of persuading. 'One of the things that's important is to decide the order you approach them. Some are harder than others, and in this case we're asking a favour. The tough ones may agree when they see the others have initialled it—but if I started with them, they wouldn't.' There were two underwriters he wanted to see this afternoon. One was in the category he'd describe as less difficult, the other was one of the tough ones.

We went over to the first box, and Michael asked the underwriter if he remembered about the co-venturer's Cost of Control risk. 'This was the small guy, if you remember, who got lumbered with $14,000.'

The underwriter looked at the slip, particularly the previous initials.

'David's done it w.p.' Michael winked at me. 'Meaning "with pleasure".'

The underwriter said he hoped I realized this was one of Michael's jokes. Really it meant 'without prejudice'. However, since he'd been having a drink with Michael at lunchtime for his birthday, he supposed he'd better write it.

Michael picked up the slip with the happy look of a schoolboy collecting autographs, and we moved on to the next box. Though he had said the underwriter would be more difficult, he turned out to be a mild-looking, grey-haired man with glasses. He began by saying that if it was like most of the risks

Michael brought him I'd better put my notebook away, because the language was likely to be pornographic.

Michael give him a disarming smile and launched into the story of the Cost of Control risk—by this time he had warmed to it, so you felt that his heart was almost bleeding for the oil company.

The underwriter, as predicted, looked doubtful. 'Have they had any claims?'

'The record's very good.' Michael looked almost hurt, as if anyone should think it hadn't been. 'And the good news is, you get some extra premium for holding them covered.'

Till now the underwriter had been making little tapping movements with his pen, in the way that underwriters often do when they don't like the sound of something. Suddenly he picked up his pen and initialled the slip. 'He's like a bloody rubber ball, isn't he?'

Michael grinned. One way and another, he seemed to be having a good birthday.

Increasingly the broker tends to see his job as part of a total service to the people who place insurance with him. 'Basically our job is getting premiums down for our clients,' says Mr W. F. Harris of Bowrings, 'but it's also part of a wider service. On fire business an ordinary insurance company isn't concerned with saving life in the same way as we are. We see it as part of our job to check that all fire alarms work and that people can get out of a building.'

Forward planning is another aspect of the broker's job which interests them at Bowrings. Recently a firm which makes duplicators was planning a new factory in Scotland, and came to Mr Harris's department to discuss the best way of building before even a brick was laid. Another example was a large group which had a consequential loss insurance, meaning that they were indemnified for loss of business following a fire. 'One day it suddenly occurred to them,' Mr Harris told me, 'that if they were put out of business for twelve months they were out of business for good. We set up a four-day conference with them to work something out, and we did so. In the end it'll probably lose us money, but it's part of the brokers' service.'

One way in which the broker can help is to advise his client on what proportion of a loss he should bear himself. Known as a deductible, this is roughly comparable to the way in which most people have to pay the first £10 of damage on an ordinary car insurance. In the case of a very large firm, Mr Harris explained, there are bound to be annual claims up to a certain figure. If the client agrees to pay these himself it means that his premium will be that much cheaper.

Recently, he told me, Bowrings had been working out an elaborate programme on these lines for a very large metal products group. 'We ran a series of computer programmes which showed that the annual losses from fire looked like being less than £40,000. If they had a deductible of £100,000 they were going to save a lot of money on the premium. The point is the premium saving has got to be greater than the losses.'

Supposing, I asked, they had fires which cost more than £40,000? Mr Harris said that if you became self-insured you had to make sure you didn't have fires. To this end, Bowrings had arranged a comprehensive survey of all the group's factories – only they had so much plant scattered around the Midlands and the north that it was a bit like painting the Forth Bridge – by the time they'd finished surveying them all, they'd have to go back to the beginning. Meanwhile if I had never seen a fire surveyor at work, would I like to see how it was done?

Which was why, next day, I found myself at a metal factory in Birmingham almost in the shadow, if it has anything as old-fashioned as a shadow, of Spaghetti Junction.

'What I've really got to do is go through this factory and see what they're doing about fire protection.'

Bernard Turner, the fire surveyor, was a relaxed, rather

quiet-voiced man in his middle thirties. He had been working on the group's factories for the last few weeks, he told me. This was one of the smaller ones, and it was his first visit.

We drove round the loops of Spaghetti Junction a few times, narrowly avoided ending up at Aston Villa football ground, and finally found the factory. Bernard Turner's appointment was with Mr Freeman, the Works Engineer, who turned out to be a short, humorous-looking man with a beard. He said he thought he ought to meet Mr Harvey, who was the Works Foreman.

Mr Harvey had a Brummie accent and the sort of lined, trustworthy look that a works foreman should have. We sat in a small glass office which was an oasis of quiet among the din of plating machines and pop music. Outside some meditative-looking Sikhs were carting round trays of brass valves on fork-lift trucks. On a series of cards in the small office were more bits of chromium, this time the finished products. What the factory made, said Mr Freeman, were valves and taps for central heating.

Bernard Turner began by explaining what the visit was all about. 'The point is, your company's decided they're going to bear the first chunk of any insurance claim. That means we want to make sure you're as well protected against fire as possible.' He spelt it out briefly and simply, then turned to a series of questions on his pad. What were the factory's hours of working, was there one person in charge of fire extinguishers, how often did they test the fire alarms, and so on. Did they, for example, ever have a practice evacuation of the premises?

Mr Freeman shook his head a bit guiltily and admitted they'd never had one.

'What about training?'

Mr Freeman shook his head again. They'd had a lecture from the fire brigade about five years ago, and he was afraid that was about all.

Bernard Turner wrote 'No training' on his pad and underlined it, then said reassuringly that a lot of other factories were not much better. All the same, it was the kind of thing, he told them amiably, that he'd recommend. Meanwhile what about machine tools that came from abroad—if there was a fire, would there be a long delay in getting replacements? This hardly seemed to be relevant to fire protection, but Bernard Turner explained that it was something all fire surveyors had to think of as a factor in consequential loss. Because the firm was also insured against loss of earnings after a fire, he had to make sure they could get things going quickly.

Presently he came to the end of his string of questions. We set off round the factory with Mr Harvey as guide.

Bernard Turner noticed that the fire extinguishers were set on red boards. 'That's good. Makes them easier to notice.' What pleased him less was a bit of frayed flex, attached to the plug of an electric kettle in the swarf shop. 'There are three main causes of fire—smoking, electrical faults and children.'

'Children?'

'They come in and set light to things for the hell of it. That's why we always ask about security arrangements.'

We went on through the plating shop where metal valves were being dipped in tanks of greenish water. 'Plating shops are mucky places but not much of a fire risk.' In the next room there were some oil tanks, with a lot of sawdust round the floor which had been put down to soak up spilt oil. Mr Turner said you could get powder which was non-combustible instead of sawdust. He didn't much fancy all that oil-soaked sawdust, if somebody broke the rules and trod out a cigarette.

What this factory really needed, though, were sprinklers. An efficient sprinkler system, which was basically a series of water jets from the roof, was far and away the safest fire protection. It could also, he added, reduce the client's premium by as much as 60 per cent.

Mr Harvey explained a bit apologetically that they had been thinking of putting in a sprinkler system of their own design.

Bernard Turner nodded sympathetically, but didn't look too happy. 'I think we should recommend you to a proper firm,' he said, as if he didn't want to hurt Mr Harvey's feelings. 'If you want a suit made you go to a tailor.'

On the way round I noticed that some of the extinguishers were marked as being for Class A or B fires. What, I asked, was the difference? Bernard Turner explained that all fire extinguishers were marked according to whether they held foam or water, and added that with a lot of non-English speaking employees around, they might have to think about re-labelling. 'A Class A fire's one you put out with water. Class B is oil—where water'll make it worse. Class C's electric—if you put water on it you're a dead man.'

We had moved on to the stores. Mr Turner looked a bit critical and said that store-rooms were always dangerous because you had such a wide collection of things, paper, packaging and so forth. One of the things he might suggest, even though it was a small room, was the installation of fireproof doors. 'Rather like bulkheads on a ship, that you can close off.' Recently, he said, Bowrings had placed the insurance on its spares department for an international airline: the whole department was completely contained in one building at Heathrow. Bowring's surveyor had gone into the problem with underwriters and the fire brigade, and brought out a plan for dividing the whole building into three compartments with fire-brick walls, and a system of sprinklers. 'You can't prove it won't catch fire,' he added. 'All the same, we shall bring down the potential loss from thirty million to a million.'

By now Bernard Turner's pad was pretty full of notes. On the way back to Mr Freeman's office I asked him if it wasn't difficult going from one sort of factory to another, and taking in so many different processes. He paused to consider an office door which he thought opened the wrong way if a lot of people were trying to get out in a hurry, then said it was surprising how quickly you got the hang of things if you were really interested in industry and had a feeling for the way people worked. Over the last six months he'd reported on most sorts of industry from a contraceptive factory to a shipyard. 'I usually get some idea of what's going on in the first ten minutes. From there it's a question of making the right approach. You don't say to somebody they've got to do this to comply with the rules—you say their business is likely to be more profitable if they do it. The other thing is that a surprisingly large number of managements really are concerned with their work people. If it's for the safety of their staff, they'll do it.'

A lot of people at Lloyd's will insure you against the more predictable disasters. Only one set of people will insure you against the unlikely ones. These are the contingency brokers, and their world is original, unique, and highly expert. Most brokers pride themselves on being large but the contingency brokers take an esoteric pleasure in being small. There is only one firm of them, Adam Brothers Contingency Ltd. It occupies a single floor of a house in one of the small streets off St Mary Axe, behind the church of St Andrew Undershaft, where they used to raise the London maypole.

To find out what goes on in the world of contingency broking, I talked to Mr J. P. Hine, the chairman. Among the more picturesque characters of Lloyd's, Mr Hine sports a twirling Edwardian moustache, still drives a vintage Bentley, and on his seventieth birthday was presented by his staff with a 110 m.p.h. BMW motorbike.

How, I asked him, would he define contingency broking? Mr Hine said the best way would be to explain how the firm had developed its special interest. The original Adam Brothers were ship-owners at Aberdeen. In 1882 they decided to become Lloyd's brokers in the marine market, mostly insuring their own ships. In the earlier part of this century the firm had found itself in the doldrums and started looking round for new men and new business. Mr Hine himself had come in in

1936 and been followed a few months later by a man called Donovan Parsons, who had already worked at Lloyd's but had left and gone to Malaya to plant rubber. He had returned to London and to Lloyd's, but an important part of his interests and talent were in the theatre. 'It was really Parsons who triggered us off,' says Mr Hine, 'because he had a talent as a lyric-writer which led to his getting to know a lot of theatre people in the West End. Parsons decided there was a form of insurance needed for when a theatrical star failed to appear, and the management lost money.'

Within a couple of years the new idea of insuring the non-appearance of stars was booming. Mr Hine reeled off a list of the people they started to insure—Gordon Harker, Leslie Henson, Raymond Massey, Jack Hulbert and Cicely Courtneidge. ('And that other chap—"Can you hear me, Mother?" He's still on the books, Sandy Powell.')

As Europe drifted towards World War II, it began to occur to other people besides theatrical impresarios that anything from a trade fair to the Royal Tournament might not happen. They took out abandonment cover with the Lloyd's underwriters who had helped Adam Brothers to start the market: the firm, added Mr Hine, had gone on from there. Almost none of their business is handled direct, but is passed on to them by other Lloyd's brokers who acknowledge their expertise. 'We don't go out to get business—the other brokers come to us. They know they can put an impossible proposition to us and we can handle it.'

While I was talking to Mr Hine, the other directors drifted in, talking about the day's business over a glass of sherry. There was Mr Hine's son Harvey, who had inherited his father's taste for fast cars, and drives regularly at Oulton Park and Silverstone; Peter Nottage, the managing director, a tall quiet man who looks like a senior diplomat; and the Hon. Mrs Liliana Archibald.

Among the several thousand brokers' men at Lloyd's, Mrs

Archibald is the only woman. In a man's world she remains feminine, friendly, but intellectually extremely high-powered. The daughter of Russian emigrés, Mrs Archibald began life as a professional historian. She has written books about Peter the Great and the Romanovs, drives a Porsche 911S, and is an expert in the field of export credit guarantee insurance, which roughly means the sort of insurance exporters take out in case their customers don't pay up.

Faced with what she clearly regarded as inevitable questions about Women's Lib, she said she didn't support them, but only because you don't get things done by creating hell. 'Once you accept that women can go to a university it's illogical to create barriers to their doing anything.' All the same, she rather relishes one underwriter's suggestion for her call-sign in the Room, which was 'Adam Brothers, Eve'.

Peter Nottage produced a list of more than sixty different classifications for contingency insurance: there was Food Poisoning and Forcible Detention, Frustration, Royal Tours (Cancellation), Kidnapping, Expeditions and Twins. There was Erroneous Duplication, which Mr Nottage said was useful if you were holding a raffle and your printer went berserk and printed the winning number five hundred times over. Forcible Detention would cover a newspaper, for example, which had correspondents who might get arrested through no fault of their own behind the Iron Curtain.

What happened, I asked, if you wanted to insure an expedition? Mr Nottage explained that an Everest expedition, for instance, could protect itself from the financial loss which would follow if it didn't get far enough to send back progress reports to its newspaper and television sponsors. On the latest Everest expedition Lloyd's had quoted a premium of 4 per cent if the climbers didn't get to the base camp, 10 per cent if they didn't get to Camp Four, and so on.

One of the most popular stories at Lloyd's in recent years is that of the explorer Wally Herbert, whose expedition crossed the Arctic on foot in 1969. Herbert was under contract to various newspapers to send them reports on his progress. Meanwhile his sponsors, the Royal Geographical Society, had taken the precaution of insuring against the expedition having to be abandoned. Indeed at one stage when he had to spend a winter in a hut near the Pole, things did look very bad for Herbert. 'What the underwriters did,' says Peter Nottage, 'was to make a sporting offer. They said they would charge a very high premium, around 20 per cent. If there was a claim they would keep the premium. If on the other hand Wally Herbert made it, they would return a big chunk of the premium.' Herbert did make it, and on his return the Committee of Lloyd's gave him a lunch. At the end of the lunch the Chairman gave him something else that Lloyd's never normally does: a cheque for a no-claim bonus.

Because of the variety of the risks they place, the brokers at Adam Brothers need expert knowledge of most kinds of insurable activities, from world politics to show business.

If it is something they don't know about, they use contacts. Recently a Canadian film company wanted to insure against bad weather holding up progress on a film being made for the 1973 centenary of the Royal Canadian Mounted Police.

Peter Nottage didn't know much about the weather in Saskatchewan where the film was being shot, so he rang up the Met. Office at Bracknell, who are one of Adam Brothers' usual sources of information, but who couldn't help in this case. They suggested the High Commissioner for Canada's Office. 'By great good luck we got on to a chap who came from within a few miles of the location,' says Peter Nottage. 'He was able to give us a complete record of the weather the film unit was likely to meet.'

One of the problems they were going to have to talk over soon, said Mr Hine, was what they were going to do about the 1974 World Cup. They were being asked to provide cover for a huge sum against the possibility that the matches might not, for any reason, be played in Munich. Since the events of the 1972 Olympics,* underwriters were naturally concerned at what might happen. Mr Nottage said a lot depended on whether the Israelis were there, and on whether the German security methods were tightened up.

'We can't go ahead on the basis of 1972,' he said. 'We must either exclude acts of terrorism or put the premiums up. That's if the market will write it at all.'

Mr Hine puffed at his pipe, sipped his Madeira and nodded. 'Are we worried about anything happening to a single team, or just the cancellation of the whole event?'

Mrs Archibald said if they were worried about single teams, wouldn't they have to think of a hijack threat? 'Or supposing there was another accident like Manchester United's—would the matches go ahead?'

Mr Nottage said he wasn't worried about an accident to a single team. It might sound a bit cold-blooded, he said, but somebody would get a bye. 'There's no weather risk and I don't think there's a single team risk. There's just this political risk, and that's what we've got to talk to underwriters about.'

After that there was a bit of discussion about a personal accident policy for a racing driver in South America. 'Somewhere where they have a currency called V. Bols,' said Harvey Hine. 'Where the hell do they have V. Bols?'

'Venezuela,' said Mrs Archibald with authority. 'They're called after Bolivar.'

Peter Nottage looked it up in the *Financial Times*, said she was quite right, and they were 11·17 to the pound today.

From V. Bols the conversation went back to racing drivers and racing cars. Somewhere in the middle of it the Chairman

* Although the abandonment risk on the 1972 Olympics was written at Lloyd's, underwriters were not financially threatened even when it seemed the Games could be cancelled. Ironically, the policy was based on the abandonment before the opening—it never occurred to anyone that the Games might begin but not be finished.

said something was like insuring gravestones under water.

Peter Nottage roared with laughter. 'Tell him that story, Guv. It's an unbelievable story.'

The Chairman said it had been a long time ago and nothing to do with contingency insurance, but there had been this chap called Bob Hill. They had had an insurance to do for a big supplier of gravestones. Bob Hill wrote a risk on a huge stack of the things, at a very low rate. The trouble was that the gravestone supplier had decided to keep them all in tanks of water. 'His idea was to keep the stones in good condition, so they were malleable. Only then there was a hell of a winter and the tanks of water froze solid and all the gravestones split. Poor old Bob Hill,' added Mr Hine with cheerful nostalgia. 'He must have lost a packet.'

We finished our sherry and went out into the winter evening.

Mr Hine put on his bowler hat, and said that in their business they were really dicing with the Almighty.

'It's a good thing He tends to be on our side,' said Mrs Archibald.

Harvey Hine got on his bike, waved and disappeared in the direction of St Mary Axe. In the precarious world of the contingency brokers you felt anything might happen, but the tower of St Andrew Undershaft was still there. There was no sign of Erroneous Duplication of the stars. Across Leadenhall Street, Lloyd's still rode, like some great ship, in the moonlight.

6
Keeping the Coffee House

'Stewart Smith, Jones. Hogg Gardner, Thompson.'

What we are listening to is perhaps the most characteristic of all sounds at Lloyd's. It is the perpetual background noise of the Room, the sound of brokers' names being intoned by the Caller from the Rostrum below the Lutine Bell. From nine-thirty in the morning till five in the afternoon it goes on. According to the Caller's intonation it can variably sound like electronic music, mediaeval plainsong or a muezzin's call to prayer.

'Willis Faber, Burroughs-Johnson.' A double-barrelled name seems to give the Caller more of an intonation to bite on: his voice goes up on the first and then down on the second syllable. John*song*—it sounds like a superior brand of tea. The tone is rhythmic, sonorous, and unique. In his red robe and velvet collar, the Caller is the direct descendant of the Kidney. But like many things at Lloyd's, calling is not done merely because it is time-honoured, but because it works.

The 258 broking firms attached to Lloyd's represent between them a total of around 3,000 brokers, any or all of whom could be milling about the Room at a given moment. Suppose an underwriter or someone else from their office wants to get hold of them? All he does is go to the Caller's rostrum and give the name of the man he wants. The Caller will then intone the names of the broking firm and the broker. The extraordinary thing is that the broker will hear it, even above the hum and babel of what is seldom less than three thousand people.

How, you may ask, does it work? Lloyd's explanation is

simple. Because the noise is going on all the time, they say, you never hear the Caller's voice at all unless it is your own name he is calling. The explanation may sound unlikely, but one broker told me he could spend all day in the Room and never be aware of the Caller. 'Then at half-past four in the afternoon he calls your own name and it's as if someone had bawled it in your ear.'

The present doyen of the Caller's craft is a large, dark man named Edward Presley. With a look of Max Bygraves and an extrovert sense of humour, you feel he is the sort of man who would be at home in show business. Indeed, he is in the London phone book as E. Presley and on occasions, he told me, there had been rather a lot of phone calls from girls thinking he was Elvis. It had taken him quite a while to convince his wife they weren't for him.

How, I asked, does anyone learn to be a Caller? Edward Presley replied that it had taken him a bit more than three months. 'You sit up there practising while the Room's empty. You get rather a lot of brickbats from the staff.'

Once you'd got the trick of it, he said, it wasn't difficult—it was a question of finding your own pitch and rhythm. 'There's one name I like, a fellow with Sedgwick Forbes. His surname's Christopherson and Christopherson's a name you can get hold of. Christ-o-ferr-son,' he intoned, taking off a bit on the last syllable. 'You can break it up and you can swing it.'

You didn't need to have a loud voice, said Mr Presley, but you did have to have a clear one. The most famous of all Callers had been a man named Walter Farrant, round about the end of the last century. Farrant had started off his career as a railway porter. 'One day a Lloyd's underwriter heard him shouting all the stations from Windsor to Waterloo, and he thought he'd make a good Caller, so he brought him in.'

Eventually Farrant had become so famous in the City that *The Times* wrote half a column about him when he retired.

I asked Mr Presley if it wasn't boring sitting up there intoning all those names, and he said it wasn't boring, but it was a bit of a strain. 'We're up there four turns a day, thirty minutes at a stretch, each turn. It doesn't sound likely, but in a busy period you can easily be calling five hundred and fifty names in half an hour. Apart from people coming and giving you the names of brokers they want, you've got to watch the telewriters. This is when people up in the gallery want a broker called, and they give it to one of the waiters up there. He puts it on the telewriter, and it comes up on the Caller's rostrum.'

He had rung the Lutine Bell when the *Flying Enterprise* went down, he told me, and for the birth of Prince Andrew. Nowadays, he said rather regretfully, they didn't ring it so much—usually only for good news, and things like the Two Minutes' Silence on Remembrance Day. You get used to people gaping at you and taking photographs, he added, as if he rather liked it. In 1961 he had been to the Vancouver Exhibition as a representative of Lloyd's, red coat, top hat, white gloves and all.

In his traditional dress and position on the rostrum, the Caller is in a sense the archetypal figure of the coffee house, spanning three hundred years of history. Meanwhile Edward Presley and his red-robed colleagues are no longer the only servants of Lloyd's. It is time now to move out from the Room and look at the Corporation.

The present Secretary General of Lloyd's is Mr C. G. Wastell, and in his office, just along from the Committee Room, you can see inscribed the names of all his predecessors. Strictly speaking, they are not his predecessors as Secretary General for the title is a very new one. But in the broader sense Mr Wastell is the modern version of the Master of the coffee house. The first name on the board is that of Edward Lloyd himself.

Following him there come the successive Masters down to 1804, in which year the office of Master of the coffee house lapsed. (Possibly it might have survived to this day had it not been for the snobbishness of a certain First Lord of the

Admiralty who resented having to correspond on shipping intelligence matters with a person he called 'a waiter'. The members of Lloyd's, with a characteristically adroit touch, replied by merely promoting the Master to the post of Secretary, in which capacity the First Lord happily continued to correspond with him.)

Thus from 1804 onwards the chief administrator of Lloyd's was known as the Secretary. Perhaps the most distinguished of the Secretaries was Colonel Hozier, who came to Lloyd's in 1872, the year after it had been made a Corporation by Act of Parliament. In his reign the staff became greatly expanded and more efficient. It was Hozier himself who was largely responsible for the spread of Lloyd's signal stations and the creation of its world-wide system of overseas agents. Later he was knighted, and indirectly added to his distinctions by becoming the father-in-law of Sir Winston Churchill.

But the reason for singling out Hozier is not so much his service to Lloyd's as the insight we can get by comparing the Corporation of today with his time. Some of his office notebooks have been preserved, and a fascinating contrast they show us. When Hozier came to Lloyd's in 1872 the staff consisted of forty-four people, most of them engaged in the sort of work done by club servants. One page of his notebooks deals with what were called 'Servants' Allowances'. In it we read, for example, that the boys cleaning inkwells would get an extra 4*s* a week. For delivering Lloyd's Intelligence to newspapers after 5.00 p.m., they would get an extra 8*s* 6*d* a week, with a special fee of 4*s* a night for Christmas, Boxing Day and Easter Monday. Cleaning the Members' lavatories rated 6*s* a week. The boy 'arranging policies', surprisingly, got only half-a-crown.

These allowances were in addition to the servants' ordinary weekly wages, which were hardly generous. Even as late as 1920 the *Daily Chronicle* carried small advertisements for 'respectable boys as messengers at Lloyd's. Wages 14*s* a week, uniform and boots supplied.'

Hozier himself, it is hard not to suspect, regarded it as a major objective to keep the wage-bill down. 'Wild will be retained on the establishment at the present rate of 17*s* 6*d* per week', runs a characteristically stern entry in the office notebook, 'but he must not expect any increase. Farrant's application for an increase of wage cannot be granted.' (This was the famous Walter Farrant, the Caller.) In 1880, we find Hozier instructing that 'in future boys shall leave the service of the Committee at 16 years of age instead of at 18 as at present'—the point being, presumably, that after 16, they would demand higher wages.

But what we do not get from Hozier's notebooks is any feeling that the Corporation staff were making a contribution to the real work being done at Lloyd's. The change over a hundred years is not simply that in his time there were forty-four people on the payroll and that there are now two thousand. The point is that nowadays the whole quality of their contribution is different.

Why, you might ask, if Lloyd's is so essentially based on individualism, does it need an organization at all? The point is that it is precisely because of the organization that the underwriter can remain an individual.

What it does, in effect, is to leave him free to get on with his underwriting.

The most obvious example of how this works is in the Audit Department. The Audit came into being as a control of the underwriters' assets and, from the public's point of view, as a guarantee of the safety of a Lloyd's policy. Yet the actual mode of the control works in such a way as to keep the bookwork, from the underwriters' point of view, to a minimum.

In an earlier chapter we saw how the underwriter, having completed his year's dealings, sends his books to be audited by an accountant approved by Lloyd's. Once the accountant has confirmed his figures, the auditor's report and certificate will go to the Audit Department on the third floor of Lloyd's.

Here, in what seems an absurdly small room to be handling a continual stream of millions of pounds and dollars, all the accountants' statements are filed and checked. The man in charge of the Audit Department, Joe Hodges, is typical of Lloyd's younger financial experts. Coming in as a junior clerk, he showed sufficient promise for the Corporation to single him out. He qualified as a chartered accountant at Lloyd's expense, and now has the handling of all the accountants' returns and statistics which come in from October onwards. 'A bit like a farmer,' he says, with a grin, 'collecting the annual harvest.'

Basically what the Audit Department does is to see that the Department of Trade and Industry gets an Audit Certificate in respect of every underwriting syndicate. This shows that the underwriter has got sufficient assets to meet his losses.

But how is it possible to tell what his future losses may be? This will have been assessed by the auditors, according to a minimum standard based on past experience and what the underwriter himself thinks he needs to meet outstanding claims. In most cases the procedure is automatic and the underwriter's own estimate is accepted, though there may be half a dozen cases a year, Joe Hodges told me, where the underwriting agent and the auditor don't agree. If this happens it is the job of the Audit sub-committee to sort it out.

Apart from the annual harvest of Audit Certificates, the Department is also responsible for much of the mountain of paper work which in a more conventional organization would clutter the underwriter's own desk. The Bank of England needs details of all the names' dollar holdings—these go direct from the Audit Office. If a name dies, there will be the question of withdrawing his deposit. This will be handled by Mr Hodges' department as well.

Often the Department has to deal with individual problems—while I was there Mr Hodges had two particular cases which he said would have to go before the Committee of Lloyd's because there was a question of principle involved.

The first concerned a name who was living in Rhodesia, which presents a special problem for Lloyd's because since UDI it has been illegal to transfer money from Rhodesia to Britain. 'The point about this particular chap,' Hodges explained, 'was that he came in as a name during the 1960s, when a lot of underwriters were making losses. It was just about the time UDI had been declared, and because of the regulations he couldn't send any money out of Rhodesia. So what happened was that the other people on his syndicate paid his claims and there doesn't seem much chance he can pay them back. He's managed to produce £5,000 from a bank account in England, but all the rest of his cash is in Rhodesia. In this case we shall ask the Committee if they'll make a grant from the Central Fund to repay the other names what he owes them.'

I asked about the other case he was preparing for the Committee and Mr Hodges said it wasn't a political one this time but rather a sad one. Somebody who'd been a clerk on a syndicate had been helped to become an underwriting member about ten years back—the underwriting agency had put up the £8,000 deposit for him to become a name. Unfortunately this had also been around the lean years of the mid-1960s. There had been quite heavy underwriting losses, and in 1971 the man had died. He'd left about £7,000 and a bungalow where his widow was living. On the other hand he owed £5,000 on his underwriting losses and another £5,000 to the underwriting agency which had lent him the money to become a name in the first place.

The story seemed to illustrate that being a name at Lloyd's is not necessarily a one-way ticket to becoming a millionaire. I remembered Henry Chester's remark about it being no good for a worrier. What, I asked Joe Hodges, would happen now?

'At the moment the situation's fairly dodgy. Naturally the underwriting agents would like to get their money back, and the Committee of Lloyd's have got to decide what to do about it. The losses will be paid all right—they'll come out of the

Central Fund. The agents say they'll write off the loan if the Committee will meet the underwriting losses. The Committee may agree—or they may say the widow must pay something towards them.'

What about the other departments of the Corporation? If you look at a list of them you will find sixteen main ones ranging from Claims to Intelligence and Aviation. Among the most recently developed on a large scale is the Information Department. In its nature Lloyd's has always mirrored world events, and nowadays with such things as hijacking and pollution stories, Lloyd's increasingly makes news.

Though Lloyd's does not advertise, one aspect of the Information Department's work is to see that journalists are informed about the often subtle intricacies of underwriting business. Pamphlets and brochures are produced in more than a dozen languages. Over 7,000 people are annually shown round Lloyd's—among them parties of provincial newspaper editors, foreign journalists and school careers masters who may be expected to introduce the underwriters of the future.

In terms of power the most important department is the Financial Comptroller's, which looks after Lloyd's various trust funds. Not all these are necessarily British-based. Sometimes an overseas government will insist that the resources to pay claims must be lodged in their own country, and if so it will be the responsibility of the Financial Comptroller's Department in London. So, too, is the money which Lloyd's invests from its various funds and deposits. 'Compared with a conventional insurance company,' I was told, 'it isn't all that much. Even so, an overnight fund of a million pounds or so—a small merchant bank would quite like to have the handling of this sort of money.'

Although the Corporation is there primarily as a service to the underwriters, it also has the job of protecting the public and seeing that Lloyd's rules are observed. In the role of watch-dog is the Advisory and Legislation Department. Its job is to check on those risks which underwriters are not allowed to write. We saw, earlier for instance, how credit insurance – meaning the guaranteeing of someone's financial stability – was banned after the Harrison case. War risks on land are also banned by agreement between all British insurers, because the amounts involved could be so astronomical that there would be no guarantee of all claims being met.

Increasingly there is also the problem of foreign legislation—although Lloyd's writes some form of insurance for every country in the world (except Rhodesia and, for some reason, North Korea) there are some countries whose national laws impose restrictions. In France, for instance, a foreign insurer can write non-marine but not marine business. Italy has a law which specifically prohibits insurance being placed with an individual as opposed to a company. This automatically excludes Lloyd's—though it remains to be seen how far such legislation will survive Britain's entry to the Common Market.

In recent years many of the developing nations have set up national insurance companies of their own with a prohibition on others. When this happens, Lloyd's reacts to the situation with a characteristic mixture of expertise and charm.

'If a country decides it's going to set up a company of its own,' one underwriter told me, 'we usually ask if they'd like any help. Quite often we'd send somebody out for a year or so to advise them on how to set up their office. There wouldn't be any strings attached, but in years to come it'd probably pay off in terms of making contacts.'

The Advisory Department also checks on some of the specific types of insurance which underwriters, for what one could call generally public-spirited and ethical reasons, are not allowed to write. Nobody can be insured at Lloyd's against the consequences of their own criminal actions—in other words if you were a burglar you wouldn't be able to get Lloyd's to insure you against breaking your leg in the line of duty.

Where anything can be even remotely held to be against the public interest, Lloyd's will not permit insurance. For instance it stays clear of disputes between capital and labour—an employer can't take up an insurance against his men going on strike, but equally a union itself cannot insure its members against loss of earnings during a strike.

The life of a head of state may not be insured, in case someone got to know what was the going rate at Lloyd's on their chances of assassination. You can insure against a General Election happening on a particular day to spoil your daughter's eighteenth birthday party, but not against the chance that the Tories or Labour might win. Political parties have been unable to insure since 1952, when Sir Eustace Pulbrook, a former Chairman of Lloyd's, wrote a policy indemnifying Liberals against the loss of electoral deposits. What disturbed the Committee of Lloyd's was not so much that underwriters had had to pay upon a trail of Liberal lost deposits. It was that they might have seemed to be encouraging a certain frivolity among candidates.

Meanwhile how are the rules enforced? Lloyd's would hardly be Lloyd's if underwriters did not occasionally find ingenious ways round them.* On the other hand if there were ever a repetition of the Harrison case, it would come to light through Lloyd's Policy Signing Office.

The Signing Office, working in conjunction with Lloyd's data-processing centre at Romford in Essex, records the details

* When they do find a way to bend the rules, it is less often because of a hunger for premiums than a feeling that someone who wants an insurance should be able to get it at Lloyd's. A broker told me he had once been asked to insure a manufacturer who planned to market some commemorative plaques for the Inauguration of a US President.

'Suddenly he realized,' said the broker, 'that there was a risk. Supposing the President got assassinated before the Inauguration? Plenty of underwriters were ready to write the risk—the only trouble was that Lloyd's may not quote a rate of odds against the death of a head of state. Eventually we came up with a policy which protected the client from loss due to cancellation of the Inauguration for any cause whatsoever. This could have included anything from earthquakes to Acts of God—as well as the one thing he was actually concerned with.'

of every policy issued. Since 1924 no policy has been recognized as valid unless it bears the official seal of the Signing Office. As they arrive from the brokers, all policies are checked by skilled examiners who will make sure there is no transgression of Lloyd's rules.

'It might be that the underwriter had inadvertently written something he was not supposed to,' explains Mr Ellington, General Manager of the Signing Office, 'or perhaps an error of a word or two that had crept in through a typing slip in the broker's office. Even in the case of such small points, the checker will query the policy—and if necessary call the broker in to discuss it and put it straight.'

Once the policy is approved it goes to the Signing Section where it gets an official seal. Meanwhile all details of the risk are recorded on the Premium Advice Card produced by the computer at Romford: a copy of this will eventually go to both broker and underwriter.

The computers may seem a little out of place in the organization of the coffee house. In another sense they are the link between three hundred years of history and the future. They are the means by which Lloyd's individualism survives in the world of modern business communications.

The present occupier of the most important position in Lloyd's is a marine underwriter named Paul Dixey. He was elected Chairman at the end of 1972, and according to precedent will probably remain in office for at least two years. In that time his influence over the whole market is likely to be considerable.

Not that Paul Dixey himself suggests any particular interest in power. He is a quiet intellectual-looking man who has the unusual quality of being as good a listener as he is a talker. What seems likely to make him an outstanding Chairman is an instinctive natural strength—an ability to see to the heart of the situation and act upon it coolly. When you meet him in the Chairman's office you sense a certain rather humorous surprise at finding himself surrounded with the impedimenta of power, the relics of Nelson and Angerstein. At the same time there is no doubt about his devotion to Lloyd's. When I asked him what he would like to have been if he hadn't worked here, he thought for a long time and then said he simply couldn't imagine himself doing anything else.

Paul Dixey was born in 1915, the son of an underwriter who was also a Chairman of Lloyd's. He read Economics and English at Cambridge and still reads widely, mostly history and modern fiction. He lives in the country at Dunmow in Essex, in a house which once belonged to H. G. Wells.

Family life, you feel, is something that matters deeply to Paul Dixey. So, perhaps more than to most underwriters, does the world outside Lloyd's. In politics he describes himself as a radical, and among his closest friends at Dunmow was the late Kingsley Martin, editor of the left-wing *New Statesman*. The day I went to see Paul Dixey a newspaper article had appeared denigrating Kingsley Martin, and Dixey had just written an angry letter to the journalist concerned, defending his friend's reputation.

Another side of him is that for five years he was a Rural Councillor at Dunmow. 'The important achievement while I was on the Council wasn't that we got a new sewerage system installed,' he said, 'but that we saw the wishes of the village people were observed. The trouble with any kind of governing is that it can obscure what people really want.'

In a way, his principles for the Dunmow Rural Council are those he applies to the chairmanship of Lloyd's. The greatest danger in the job, he believes, is to get out of touch with the people doing the real work in the market. One previous Chairman had told him that he thought all members of the Committee ought to have lunch every day in the Captains' Room, and it was the best piece of advice he'd ever been given. 'People won't come up to the chairman's office to tell you you're making a mess of things, but they will if they meet you at the lunch table. It's important that the people who are actually running the coffee house should be seen around.'

On the broader level the Chairman's job, he said, was to be a sort of ambassador for Lloyd's. When I saw Mr Dixey, Britain had just joined the European Community. Over the coming year, he felt, an important part of his job would be to tour the other countries of the Community explaining to their governments and insurance people exactly what Lloyd's was, and how it worked. Sometimes a new or emergent country would pass new laws which made it difficult for Lloyd's to write business, and in that case his role was to try to smooth the way for any adjustment in their laws which would make it possible. Before he became Chairman one of his own experiences of this kind had been a famous episode when a group of Lloyd's underwriters had saved the market a huge loss by freeing some ships which had been seized by the Indonesian government (*see* Chapter 9).

Was Lloyd's, I asked, likely to see considerable reforms during his period of office?

Mr Dixey said that an important point about being Chairman was that you had to reflect the needs of the moment—it was no use being a reforming Chairman if you happened to come in at a moment when the market didn't want to reform. His own predecessor, Sir Henry Mance, had been responsible for some of the most important changes of the decade, including the admission of women members. What the market needed now was a time of consolidation.

Ultimately he said there was one basic rule for any Chairman. 'We're here to run the coffee house properly, and to see that underwriters' interests are looked after. If there are obstacles in the way of their work, and we can help remove those obstacles, then it's our job to do so. What we *aren't* here to do is tell the underwriters how to run their business.'

This is a meeting of the Committee of Lloyd's. It is not a

particularly dramatic event—indeed it is a rather low-key one. If it were not for the setting of chandeliers and the seascape over the Adam fireplace, it could be the meeting of a moderate-sized town council. Indeed, in a sense, it is just that, for the Committee of Lloyd's looks after the working lives of a community of around 7,000 people. For all the low-key impression, this is the real centre of power in Lloyd's.

Because Lloyd's believes in energy and new blood, no one stays on the Committee more than four years. The sixteen members are elected from the whole body of the market, underwriters and brokers. Looking round the mahogany table I notice Mr Eliot, the aviation underwriter, for once without his tin of humbugs. There is a small man smoking a pipe who is the biggest reinsurance underwriter in the business, and who spends his weekends digging on archaeological sites threatened by a new motorway in Bedfordshire.

At the middle of the table are three high-backed chairs, for the Chairman and the two Deputy Chairmen who usually remain in office about two years. Along the wall behind them sit the Secretary General and about eight of the senior Corporation staff who are on hand to advise the Committee on matters relating to their own departments.

What the Committee is discussing at the moment is a rather technical question. An underwriting syndicate has applied to admit a non-member of Lloyd's as a partner. It seems the rule is that 75 per cent of the voting shares must be in the name of members. 'I seem to remember that in law there's no such thing as a sleeping partner.' The underwriter with a taste for archaeology looks up. Somebody else says didn't they go into all this in Cromer (the Cromer Report, *see* Chapter 10), then a dark stocky man opposite the Chairman says that speaking as a simple soul, which he clearly isn't, he thinks it all sounds a bit dubious.

Most of the rest of the Committee seem to share his doubts. 'I don't think they can do it like this,' says the Deputy Chairman firmly. 'We don't want to be obstructive, but it looks like a point of principle. I suggest we put it back to them, and see if they can think of a variation.'

Almost at once the discussion has moved on: the Committee are being asked to approve a Salvage Award for a ship which got into difficulties when her cargo of caustic soda caught fire somewhere off the coast of the Spanish Sahara. Both seem equally remote from the Committee room, with the chandeliers glittering pink and blue and the London November sky outside.

Evidently there is no problem about the Salvage Award and we move on to the next item. This time Joe Hodges of the Audit Department goes and sits next to the Chairman. I listen with increased interest—this is the question of the two names he told me about earlier, the man in Rhodesia and the other one.

'This is a matter of being in default on Audit?' It must have happened before, you feel, but the Committee all look pained.

The Chairman says he knows a bit about this case, and he doesn't really see what they can do. 'Morally,' he says, 'this man's broke. At least he's politically broke. I think we've got to agree a grant from the Central Fund. Otherwise it's not fair to the other names.'

There seems to be a general assent, and Joe Hodges moves on to his next item. This is about the man who died before he had paid off his underwriting losses and the debt to his underwriting agent. The Committee listen to Joe Hodges sympathetically, and the Chairman nods.

'Really the situation is that if we say the estate's got to pay up, it means the widow's homeless?'

Joe Hodges says he thinks there'd be a bit of money, but not much. The widow might be able to get a mortgage on her bungalow.

'Even so, I don't think we could sell the roof over her head. I wouldn't like to do that.' I notice a general hum of approval.

Joe Hodges goes back to his seat by the wall looking pleased. Even accountants, you feel, are human.

After this the next question is the admission of names—attached to the agenda is a list of those who have come in front of the Rota Committee over the last month. Among them, I notice, those of Mrs May and the Irishman. At this stage, admission is almost automatic unless the Chairman of the Rota Committee has any doubts.

On this list it seems he has doubts about one of them: one of the potential names had borrowed money from his brother to increase his reserves, and the security he had given his brother was his own house.

'I suppose we could put a means test on him every year?' The Committee sound anxious to be fair, but concerned about it. In the end they decide the Rota Committee had better get a few more facts.

Meanwhile, because the admission of names has to be approved by vote, one of the secretaries from the Corporation staff is going round with a small bowl containing what look like mothballs, then goes to the side table where there is a small box with two drawers and a hole in the middle. One of the senior Corporation staff sitting next to me explains that this is the traditional method of voting—the members have to put the mothball-like objects into one of the drawers. (Once a new Committee member thought it must be some curious ritual of offering sweets round, so he put the mothball in his mouth and sucked it.)

Presently the voting is complete. All the names are admitted, except the one the Rota Committee Chairman was going to write to. There is some discussion about the proposed re-organization of the Audit Department, then the Committee meeting is over.

On the way out Mr Dixey stops me and says he's afraid it hasn't been very exciting, but then it isn't meant to be.

'After all, we're only keeping the coffee house.'

The waiter opens the mahogany door and the Committee file out. I recall something said by one of the eighteenth-century Masters of the coffee house, Thomas Taylor: 'The management of this house has ever been the pride of my heart.'

Today, nearly two hundred years later, his words are still true for the Committee and Corporation.

7
'Report Me to Lloyd's'

If you take the quiet by-lane that leads from Dover Castle to St Margaret's Bay, you will scarcely notice a small track going off it. At first the track seems to lead nowhere in particular, then you find yourself climbing.

In a few moments you are looking at the most historic coastal view in England—Dover Castle and the looming grandeur of Shakespeare Cliff, the monument which marks the departure point of Bleriot's famous flight to France. Nearer to you is another monument, this time the tall obelisk erected to the memory of the Dover Patrol. Perched on a sort of eyrie in the cliff beside it, there is a small white building with a big window looking across the Channel.

This is the Dover Straits Coastguard Station at Lethercote Point, centre of all search and rescue operations in the world's busiest marine highway. If there is any vessel in trouble, it will be the coastguards on duty here who will press the 'scramble' button to the helicopters at Manston, or call out the lifeboats from the North Foreland to Beachy Head.

Overhead, the radar scanner swings. Lethercote Point is also the traffic control for the Channel. If a vessel moves out of its lane or breaks the keep-right rule, it will show on the radar screen and a warning will go out.

Meanwhile, at the big control desk, the two coastguards on duty keep continual watch. Presently a small cargo boat looms out of the in-shore mist, and one of them looks at her through the telescope. '*Sennar*. Sudan Lines.' He writes the name in a book, then lets me look through the telescope, and I get a glimpse of cars and lorries loaded on her deck.

In the background the crackle of radio goes on—coastguard station radios are always tuned to 2182 metres. This is the frequency all ships use. Having made contact on 2182 metres, they will then turn to another frequency to leave it clear for distress messages.

'This is the *Westminsterbrook*. Calling 2182. Calling *Winchesterbrook*.' The coastguard in charge nods, and says they'll be sister ships, wanting to get in touch with each other. There is a hum and a crackle and a polite Dutch voice saying good evening, he is Scheveningen Radio, and what is their working frequency?

Outside it is dark now. Straight ahead through the window the North Goodwin Lightship has begun to flash. In the radar room the operator moves away from studying his screen, ships showing as specks of light in the darkness like a maritime Milky Way. He begins talking on the radio, dictating a warning about a marker buoy that has broken adrift somewhere near Boulogne. 'Boulogne,' he repeats, spelling it out. 'Golf November Echo.' At the main control desk the other coastguard writes down the details of a motor yacht whose owner has just phoned in to say he is leaving Dover for Southampton, and will the coastguards note his description and time of arrival. This is the small change of shipping information, part of the constant stream of detail pouring out across a thousand crackling radios. What has it all to do with Lloyd's? To see that, we must go back to the earliest days of the coffee house.

'If anybody wants to know something about a ship or the sea, they come to us. To the ordinary person, Lloyd's means ships.'

These words, spoken by a Lloyd's agent in a West Country port, seemed to define what has come to be an almost unconscious connection: for two hundred years at least, Lloyd's has been regarded as the main source of all shipping information. Even in Edward Lloyd's time, *Lloyd's News* had been the main foundation of the coffee house's success. Though it ceased publication in 1697, Lloyd continued to issue shipping information whenever he had news of interest. Thus when the *News*' successor, *Lloyd's List*, appeared in 1734, there was a tradition to build on.

Even so, the actual published material was only the tip of the iceberg. By the end of the eighteenth century Lloyd's shipping knowledge was already regarded with awe in Whitehall. At least once in the Napoleonic Wars the Committee were able to give the Admiralty the first news that French ships had been sighted, off Cromer. When the British ship *Hopewell* was captured off Lowestoft in 1794 – Lloyd's intelligence service seems to have been particularly efficient off the East Coast – they were able to inform the Admiralty, who in turn asked what convoy the *Hopewell* had sailed in. The Committee of Lloyd's, with due respect, told the Admiralty that she had not been in convoy at all, but they could give the name of the French vessel which had captured the *Hopewell*, not to mention from what port she had sailed and how many other British prizes she had taken.

In other ways Lloyd's had become recognized as an administrative power. If a naval captain wanted to complain of disobedience from merchant ships in convoy, he would contact Lloyd's rather than the Admiralty. Once, the Committee got to know of inadequate convoy arrangements at Falmouth. They passed the information to the First Lord, who dealt with it promptly. In the late 1790s, the relationship was such that Angerstein could write to the Admiralty Secretary to request that a ship of the line be stationed off Ostend, to protect the passage of a number of valuable merchantmen. By 1804, writes Angerstein's biographer, the coffee house was 'an empire within itself; an empire which, in point of commercial sway, variety of powers, and almost incalculable resources, gives law to the trading part of the universe'.

Meanwhile there had been one other event which would eventually lead to Lloyd's acquiring its most famous piece of hardware: the loss, in 1799, of the frigate *Lutine*. Originally launched at Brest in 1785, the *Lutine* had been one of sixteen French warships surrendered to Admiral Hood at Toulon in 1793. Her French name is roughly translatable as 'Sprite', but for some reason the British Navy, having acquired her, kept the French one. In her new role as HMS *Lutine* she was attached to the Mediterranean Fleet and was part of a frigate squadron under Nelson's command in 1794.

The *Lutine*'s next and most dramatic appearance in history came in 1799. In that year a number of British merchants in Hamburg found themselves pushed for credit as a result of the Napoleonic Wars. The London banks decided to send a cargo of bullion for their support, and asked the Admiralty to loan them a ship. The only one which happened to be available was the *Lutine* and she sailed from Yarmouth for Hamburg on October 9 under the command of Captain Lancelot Skynner. Included in her cargo there were nearly 42,000 Spanish silver *pistoles*, 58 bars of gold, and 81 double and 138 single gold *Louis*.

What happened then is an odd and slightly sinister story. For some reason, never discovered, she went off course. Around midnight on October 9 she struck the sands at the entrance to the Zuider Zee and sank in nine fathoms of water with the loss of all hands. Various theories have been put forward to account for why a ship bound for Hamburg should have gone aground in the Zuider Zee. There was, it is true, a north-westerly gale on the night in question. There are also stories of riotous celebrations among the officers before they left Yarmouth, and even a mysterious rumour that the *Lutine* was secretly carrying the Dutch crown jewels.

Meanwhile the whole of her valuable cargo had been underwritten at Lloyd's, and the underwriters paid their losses promptly. The possibilities of salvage looked slight, since the Netherlands government claimed that the loss had been in their territorial waters. When, in 1801, a Dutch fisherman named

Wyck brought up £83,000-worth of bullion, they claimed two-thirds, though they returned some silver spoons which had belonged to Captain Skynner to the dead man's father, and a sword made for the first lieutenant. It was identified by the mark of the maker, one Cullen, the King's cutler, of Charing Cross.

More attempts to raise the cargo came to little or nothing. There were protracted negotiations between Lloyd's and the Dutch government in 1814, 1821, and again in 1857. In 1859, divers working under the protection of a Dutch gunboat recovered £22,000-worth of bullion, the ship's bell and her rudder, which has since been carved into a chair and can be seen in the writing-room at Lloyd's.

The 80-lb bell itself, mounted on its wrought-iron frame, dominates the Room behind the Caller's rostrum. It is still possible to discern on it the date it was made, the crown and arms of the house of Bourbon, and also the inscription *St Jean*, which may have referred to the *Lutine*'s patron saint. Though its historic function of sounding the loss of a ship has virtually ceased, it is still the most famous visible symbol of Lloyd's.

As for the rest of the *Lutine* treasure, it was estimated in 1859 that a million pounds' worth of gold bars, Spanish *pistoles* and *Louis d'or* still lay buried beneath the shifting sands at the entrance to the Zuider Zee. Today, more than a century later, the *Lutine*'s golden treasure seems likely to remain there.

By the middle part of the nineteenth century there had been a considerable spread of Lloyd's 'almost incalculable resources'. It might be Lord Palmerston asking the Committee of Lloyd's to advise him how the British consul at Le Havre could recover nine guineas he had spent on helping the master of a schooner. It might be the Royal Society asking if Lloyd's could identify a curious bottle found in the River Ob in Siberia. (Lloyd's, with almost irritating expertise, were able to tell them that it was a device used by Norwegian fishermen as a float for their nets.)

Meanwhile in 1852 the Committee of Lloyd's had taken an important step to augment its communications service. It had begun to set up a chain of signal stations around the British coast. Partly this was to help underwriters, but it had a much wider use for merchants. In those days a ship might arrive from America or Australia without knowing which European port was currently paying the best price for her particular cargo. Thus the master of a British ship arriving in the Channel would signal her name and ask to be reported to Lloyd's. She would then lie off the coast, waiting for orders as to which port to proceed to.

The result was that Lloyd's signal stations became part of Britain's coastal landscape. If you walk to the top of Beachy Head today, you may sit on a bench enclosed by a low stone wall. On it, there is an inscription recording that it was originally part of a signal station belonging to Lloyd's of London. The people of the Lizard, writes Gibb, 'when they speak of Lloyd's, mean not the great building in Leadenhall Street but a little, squat, storm-beaten house on the cliff's edge which for half a century greeted English sailormen with their first welcome home'.

By 1883 the number of Lloyd's signal stations had grown to thirteen. By the end of the century it was nearly forty. Much of the expansion was due to Colonel Hozier, who as Secretary of Lloyd's had toured the coastline of England buying up land for the stations. Even so, by 1896 their day was almost over. In that year Marconi made his first radio transmission over nine miles, and signalling would soon be outmoded as a method of communication with ships at sea.

Of Hozier's original forty, only the one at Gibraltar still survives as a working signal station: ships entering the Mediterranean will still ask, in the old phrase, 'Report me to Lloyd's'. The Gibraltar station proved its continuing usefulness in the spring of 1973, when it helped to track a German vessel suspected of carrying arms for the IRA. The ship, thanks largely to the Gibraltar signal station's help, was eventually arrested on the coast of Ireland.

Meanwhile, since 1811, there had been another link in the chain of Lloyd's communications. This was the setting up of the system of agents. From the earliest days underwriters had had their own contacts in foreign ports who could help with the survey of ships and cargoes, but it had been a purely informal arrangement.

Now, since 1811, these informal contacts had been put on a more official basis. Underwriters wanting information about a ship or cargo in a foreign port would channel their queries through the local Lloyd's agent, who would also provide the market with information of sailings and arrivals.

By 1829, Lloyd's had appointed over 350 agents in the world's ports, mostly shipping brokers or traders whose day-to-day work would bring them in touch with shipping matters.

Today, movements in the world's ports are reported by Lloyd's agents back to Lime Street, and a million and a half of them a year will appear in the pages of *Lloyd's List*. The Intelligence Service has greatly grown, so that its world network of communications includes coastguards, radio stations and sea-rescue posts in every country. Whether or not she is insured at Lloyd's hardly a move by any ship goes unrecorded.

Today, as always, Lloyd's means ships. More than ever today, it means their safety.

On a winter Sunday morning the City of London has a certain derelict charm. There is a sense of space, like seeing a normally crowded Mediterranean beach in the early morning. For once you can see the City's geography, the streets radiating from the Royal Exchange, the network of tiny alleys which were once the homes of the coffee houses. It is a world populated by policemen and the occasional milk float.

In the deserted canyon-like streets there is hardly a lighted window, but on one of the upper floors of Lloyd's old building in Lime Street there is a row of them—the offices of Lloyd's Intelligence Department.

Its nerve centre – and this is why even on a winter Sunday morning the windows in Lime Street are lighted – is a small room equipped with telex machines which provide a round-the-clock clearing house of information of every kind to do with the world's shipping.

What was actually happening in the telex room on this particular Sunday morning? The appointment I had was with Mr Ben Cotton, who was described as the Evening Senior. I would find him, I was told by the waiter on weekend duty at the door, on the second mezzanine floor. Mr Cotton turned out to be a cheerful, laconic sort of man in his mid-thirties. Normally, he told me, all intelligence staff work one weekend in three, and he liked to do his Sunday mornings the same weekend as he was on in the evenings. That was why he was called the Evening Senior.

With him was a young man called David Watson, who was called a Deputy Evening Senior. On the whole, they said, there didn't seem to be much happening at the moment, though they'd had a hell of a week with gales round the English coast. Presently they took me into the small, partitioned area where the telex machines were. Most of what was coming over at this stage, said Ben Cotton, was pure routine.

'These are the lists of vessels coming in from Lloyd's agents in every port. They tell us what ships have arrived, and which ones have sailed. All that information will go into Monday morning's edition of *Lloyd's List*.' I glanced at the telex, sometimes twenty or so names of ships under the heading of their respective ports: Blyth, Lübeck, Genoa. Presently one of the other machines started up, printed off a couple of names, then stopped—I noticed that these were the sailings from Littlehampton. If you were going to make a list of the world's ports, I thought, you could hardly get more exhaustive.

Back in the other office David Watson was working on a

cable to send to some tug-owners in Piraeus. On the overnight information there had been a ship called the *Verona* which had developed boiler trouble soon after leaving port. She hadn't been in any sort of danger but she had needed a tow. Lloyd's had put out a message on the telex to three or four tug-owners at Piraeus. Now the *Verona* had radioed to say she had been taken safely under tow at one-forty-five. Lloyd's would report back to the other tug-owners that no further action was needed.

'Unless he didn't like the look of them, the master will have taken the first tug to get there,' explained David Watson. 'There isn't anything in it for Lloyd's, except that if the ship had got in real trouble, we might have saved the underwriters some money.'

Another ship, the *Santa Maria,* had been blown off course in the night off Nova Scotia with a disabled rudder. The night-duty man had sent a telex to tug-owners at New York, Halifax and New Brunswick. 'There's probably about four lots of tugs all steaming to her now,' he said with a grin. 'Tug-owning's a cut-throat business.'

While David Watson had been talking to me the girl operating the telex machine had come in for Mr Cotton. There was a message she thought he ought to see from Crossa at Etel, on the French Atlantic coast. She gave him the telex sheet, which was about a ship called the *Nashira*: it was in English, which is the language generally used by sea-rescue agencies. According to the telex the *Nashira* had left Rouen on November 29 and 'must arrive', the telex said, at Casablanca on December 11. The message also said she had hit bad weather.

Mr Cotton scratched his head a bit and said that today was only the 9th and he didn't quite see what they meant by 'must arrive', unless it was not a very good translation of *doit arriver*, which would probably mean 'due to arrive'. On the other hand he said you couldn't ignore a message from Crossa, which stood for Centre Regionale Operationel de Surveillance et de Sauvetage Zone Atlantique, the French sea-rescue service. What he would have to do was try to contact the owners, and see if she really was overdue. If so the owners would probably ask Lloyd's to authorize a broadcast search.

Meanwhile David Watson had been engaged in consulting what appeared to be a small library of shipping information. He had found the *Nashira*, he said, and the owners had agents in Rotterdam.

'In that case we'd better try and raise them.' Ben Cotton wrote down the name of the ship's agent, then went into the telex room. A few minutes later he came back. 'No reply. It doesn't look as if they work on Sundays.'

'So what are you going to do now?'

'We'll have to get back to Etel, and see who initiated the enquiry. If they think a search is necessary, we'll take the responsibility for alerting Lisbon Radio and Corunna.'

By now the atmosphere had begun to sharpen up a bit. You wouldn't have said their mood was tense, but there was an extra something in their voices. It didn't sound as if there was necessarily anything wrong, Ben Cotton said, but after last week's Atlantic weather you couldn't afford to take chances. While we were waiting for the girl to get the telex machine set up, I asked him whether they felt involved personally when there was a question of ships in trouble. On the whole, he told me, it came to be a matter of routine, though it was something Lloyd's prided itself on as a service. 'We've got the facilities here in the first place because of the market, but we're not doing it *for* the market.'

By now the telex operator was ready, and he started dictating rather rapidly. 'Here Lloyd's London. Refer your message overdue vessel *Nashira.* Would you please inform who initiated request. Is vessel overdue at Casablanca. Do you want me to initiate broadcast for vessel either by Corunna or Lisbon.'

The girl stopped typing, and immediately a faint ringing sound came from the telex.

'Will there be a reply this time?'

Ben Cotton nodded. 'There's bound to be one this time. The bell will stop when they begin to reply. Come on, come on,' he said impatiently, and just then the bell did stop. The telex began to write rather precariously, as if someone was picking it out with one finger.

'The vessel's owner has received one message from Corunna Radio yesterday evening.'

The telex seemed to hover for a moment, then stopped again. 'Sounds as if it's an operator who doesn't know English very well,' said Ben Cotton. 'You'd think they'd have someone experienced on.' All the same it seemed odd, the thought of somebody sitting at a rescue centre on some French cliff, tapping out words that we were reading on a Sunday morning in Lime Street.

'The vessel was due to arrive at Casablanca on December 5. But because of poor weather she was at anchorage near Ushant.'

'I wish he'd tell us whether she's still overdue or whether she's safe.' Ben Cotton began to dictate again, but meanwhile the red lines of incoming telex had started clicking.

'Our message only informs you of the overdue.'

'Apparently the vessel is safe?' Although he had said he didn't get involved, he looked relieved.

'Yes, sure.'

'Thanks very much.'

Lloyd's, it occurred to me as the girl switched off the telex, must be the only business organization in the world which incidentally helps to save life.

That, too, is part of the tradition.

Not all the stories which flicker through the Lime Street telex have such happy endings. It may seem unthinkable that a vessel of 2,000 tons could be lost in the busiest shipping lane in the world without trace or warning. But that is what happened to the Greek cargo ship *Gold Coin*. On the night of 3 December 1972 she left Rotterdam, bound for Dakar with a cargo of maize. On the second night of her voyage she struck one of the worst gales ever recorded in the Channel, a night when even a naval officer, whose destroyer was bound for Chatham, recalled that his ship had practically stood on end in the Straits.

No Channel boats had been able to cross that night, but on the 5th the morning ferry battered her way over from Boulogne. In mid-Channel her master sighted what looked like a half-deflated life-raft. He reported this to the Dover coastguards at Lethercote Point.

Ironically, the Dover coastguards knew nothing about the *Gold Coin*, but were getting seriously worried about another vessel. This was the Dutch coaster *Noblesse* which had been due in Dover Harbour early that morning from the Port of London. A gang of dockers had been engaged to unload her cargo from 8.00 a.m.

Two hours later there was still no sign of the *Noblesse*. The Dutch owner's Dover agent had become worried and contacted the Dover coastguards. They, in turn, sent a telex to the Port of London, only to learn that the *Noblesse* had sailed at 10.00 p.m. the previous evening.

Thus as soon as they got the message from the master of the Channel ferry they immediately linked the floating life-raft with the *Noblesse*. Obviously the next step was for the Dover coastguards to initiate a search. Apart from sending out their own helicopter from Manston, they also, as a matter of routine, got in touch with Lloyd's.

Would Lloyd's Intelligence initiate a broadcast enquiry? Within minutes, the broadcast had gone out. Meanwhile Lloyd's, on their own initiative, contacted the Rotterdam owners for a full description of the ship, the colour of her hull, number of masts and funnel markings. One coastguard explained to me that this can often be Lloyd's key role in a search—to tell the searchers exactly what they are looking for. 'If Lloyd's tell us she's got a crew of eight and we've picked up seven,' he told me, 'then we know we've still got one more man to look for.'

But on that morning in the gale-swept Straits there was to be no such happy ending—almost at once the Manston helicopter reported seeing four dead bodies on the life-raft. There was nothing to be done except make what seemed a hopeless search for the rest of the crew. At Lethercote Point, Station Officer William Barnes and another coastguard spent the whole day scouring the beach and clifftop, looking for a sight of wreckage. Meanwhile the Dover lifeboat went out on its grim task of picking up the four bodies from the life-raft.

Till now the Dover rescuers had been working on what seemed an obvious conclusion—that the life-raft had belonged to the *Noblesse*. But now something happened which threw an entirely new element into the situation. The North Foreland coastal radio station had come up with an answer to Lloyd's broadcast enquiry. The *Noblesse*, they said, was nowhere near the Dover Straits. She had sheltered from the gale almost immediately after leaving the Port of London, and was now lying safely at anchor in the Thames Estuary.

If there is one shaft of light in the whole dark story, it was the pleasure that Lloyd's could take in contacting the Dutch owners to tell them the *Noblesse* was safe: you can read the actual exchange of telegrams in Plate 20. But meanwhile if the life-raft was not from the *Noblesse* what ship was it from?

By now Lloyd's had discovered something else, which was that during the night of December 4, the North Foreland radio station had heard what is known as an auto-alarm on their radio. Roughly an auto-alarm is a bit like a burglar alarm. On a small ship, the radio operator will have no relief, and yet must take occasional periods of rest. Before going below to get a sleep or a meal, he will switch on his auto-alarm. If any ship in the vicinity is sending out a distress message, his auto-alarm will send off a warning signal, a bit like the noise of a police car's siren, on frequency 2182. Coastguards and other ships will take it as a preliminary warning. All radio operators who hear it will immediately clear the frequency for a distress message.

The snag with the auto-alarm is that it can often be a false one—the Dover coastguard told me that they frequently get several bursts of auto-alarm in a day, because radio apparatus may be faulty. 'When a sparks is going below for a meal,' they explained, 'he switches on his auto-alarm and tests it. That means it'll go off for a few seconds, rather as you might test an alarm clock.'

Was this what happened with the auto-alarm heard by the North Foreland radio? Or was it a genuine distress signal, the only one ever given by the stricken *Gold Coin*?

Probably the true facts will never be known—but later it was found that the watches on the drowned sailors' wrists roughly tallied with the time when the auto-alarm had sounded. And the SOS had been preceded by the call-sign SXZB.

SX is the call-sign for a Greek vessel—the last two letters, ZB, should have denoted the name of the ship, but when Peter Bingham, of Lloyd's Intelligence, looked it up in the list of call-signs there was no ZB.

Lloyd's Intelligence Department began checking the movements of all Greek ships in the area. 'It took us all morning,' says Bingham, 'before we eventually tracked her down as the *Gold Coin.*' Even so, the clinching proof did not come till Bingham managed to contact the *Gold Coin*'s owners. Could they, he asked, give Lloyd's the serial number of her life-rafts? They could, and it was identical with the one brought in at Dover.

All the resources of modern sea-rescue had not been enough to save the *Gold Coin*. Yet her story is not an entirely dark one, for it shows the interlocking pattern of communications which exists to save life at sea. In that pattern Lloyd's Intelligence plays a big part. Even when tragedy strikes, it can at least establish the facts. As a result of evidence given by Lloyd's Intelligence staff at the inquest on the *Gold Coin* victims, steps have been taken to tighten up world regulations concerning call-signs.

Meanwhile there is another link in the chain of information

which daily pours into Lime Street. This is the world-wide work of Lloyd's home and foreign agents.

'Gum arabic.' Captain Downs, who works for the Lloyd's agent at Hull, picked up the piece of yellow, rather quartz-like substance and tapped it on his desk. 'It's the stuff they put in fruit gums. Doesn't taste of anything itself, but it does when they melt it down and flavour it.'

I sniffed the hard yellow substance and handed it back. What, I asked, had gum arabic to do with being a Lloyd's agent?

He grinned and said there was practically nothing that didn't sooner or later come the way of Lloyd's agents. It might be somebody ringing up in the middle of the night to say there was a floating log in the Humber, or it might be a lady who had lost track of her son who was at sea and thought Lloyd's would be able to help her find him. 'As a matter of fact,' he added as an afterthought, 'we usually can.'

Meanwhile he wouldn't be surprised if there were one or two calls this morning—it had been foggy in the river since dawn, and now by midday it was getting worse. They got most sorts of bad weather in Hull including fog: one of the local sayings was that down by the river you could shovel it.

Captain Alan Downs was at sea himself for thirteen years till he came to this job in 1958. The firm he works for now is called Brown Atkinson. One of the oldest-established ship brokers in Hull, they have been Lloyd's agents, according to the plaque in his office, since 1857.

'In those days the firm used to run a fleet of whalers of their own.' He looked up rather nostalgically at the pictures of ships on the wall. Brown Atkinson's looks as you feel a shipping office should—huge old-fashioned desks and a picture of King Haakon on the wall of the outer office because Mr Fenton, the managing director, is also the Norwegian consul.

Although his door is marked 'Surveyor', Captain Downs

explained that he looks after everything to do with the Lloyd's agency side of the business. This means he covers an area from Flamborough to the south bank of the Humber. There are also a couple of sub-agents at Goole and Bridlington, whose job is mostly reporting casualties and shipping movements. When he sends in his daily telex list of shipping movements to Lime Street, these will be included, though the greater part will be from the port of Hull itself.

If there are casualties, Captain Downs will usually hear of them through the local tug-owning firm—though in general terms, he said, an agent isn't likely to be one of the earliest sources of casualty news. The sort of thing where he did help was when the Intelligence Department had lost track of a ship. He had sent a telex only that morning about a ship which had sailed for Hull from Tynemouth nearly a fortnight before. The Intelligence Department had been worried when she hadn't been reported as arriving at Hull—he had made a few enquiries and found that in fact she had gone straight to dry-dock, which meant that she wouldn't have been reported as an arrival in the usual way.

Otherwise Captain Downs's main job is surveying casualties. Mostly this means cargoes—in the case of damage to ships themselves, he said, Lloyd's agents both at home and abroad would call in a marine surveyor. What Captain Downs does do is to see a cargo on which there may be a claim. If a fire breaks out in the ship's hold, the consignee of the cargo will get in touch with him as Lloyd's agent, and ask him to assess the damage.

Captain Downs stressed that it is not part of his job to get involved in liability, but simply to get a survey done efficiently and quickly. 'We haven't seen the policy and we don't want to see it. If we did, it wouldn't be so easy to be impartial.'

Apart from fires in the hold, I asked, what sort of cargoes did things go wrong with?

He said the difficulty was to think of a cargo which didn't have things go wrong with it. Once he had had to survey a lot of tinned pineapples that had been loaded in Singapore, and by the time they had got to Hull, they'd been cooked. 'When we opened the tins the juice had begun to ferment and the fruit was brown. The trouble was they'd been stowed too close to the boilers.'

One of the first jobs he had ever had was to meet a man who was an interpreter in the wholesale food business. He had imported a cargo of liver sausage from Germany, and insured it with a German company who had appointed Lloyd's agent to represent them in the case of a query.

'By the time it got to Hull,' recalled Captain Downs, 'there was more than a query. The sausage had gone all mouldy, with a sort of fur sticking to it. The Port Health people wouldn't let him sell it, even if anyone would have bought it, so they asked me to go along and see it. I suppose being new to the job I let him talk me into it, but I agreed to go back and see him next day. When I got there it was all beautiful—he'd taken it home and cleaned it and sprinkled French chalk on it. We didn't let him get away with it, but the point was he knew the German insurers wouldn't pay up. He'd told them he was going to transport the cargo in cold storage, but he hadn't. He'd let it go as ordinary cargo because he didn't want to pay the extra.'

How often, I asked, was an agent able to save the underwriters money? Captain Downs said it wasn't primarily what an agent was there for, but it happened quite often. 'That bit of gum arabic I showed you just now – that was part of the cargo that came here from Port Sudan. When it got to the wharf it smelt of mothballs, so we had it tested by chemists. It had been contaminated by naphthalene gas.'

I wondered how naphthalene gas could have got into gum arabic, and Captain Downs grinned. They'd had quite a job finding that out, he said, till he had discovered that the gum arabic had been stowed near some Ethiopian hides, which were being imported to make handbags. 'I'd dealt a good deal in hides at one time, for a local tanner, and I remembered reading something about Abyssinian sheepskin. When I looked it up in *Lloyd's Survey Handbook* it said Abyssinian rawhides were always prepared for shipment with naphthalene as a protection against vermin.'

Even so, Captain Downs added, that hadn't solved the problem, though it was a good example of how an agent had to be a bit of a detective. Meanwhile he had still been stuck with 3,000 bags of gum arabic that smelt of mothballs. What he had done was to rent a warehouse and ventilate the bags by stacking them separately and leaving all the doors of the warehouse open. In the end they'd got rid of the smell and the chemists had pronounced the cargo free of naphthalene. It had been a fairly rough-and-ready method but it had saved the underwriters around £60,000.

On the other hand there were quite a lot of cases where you could only get a small proportion of salvage money back for the underwriter—would I like to see the *Marbella*, a trawler that had come in two days ago with a cargo that was going to have to be used as fishmeal? Most of the shipment had been taken out of her holds by now, but they would still be working on her – provided we could see anything – at the Hull Fish Quay.

We got in his car and drove through the fog that was circling the cold air like smoke from a bonfire. When we got down to the dock it was even thicker. The bow of the trawler loomed out, a dim blur of light coming from the sort of gantry they have at football grounds. On her decks you could see everything covered with reddish rust, great lengths of steel hawser and floats the size of beach balls.

'They've been through a hell of a time,' said Captain Downs. 'Twenty-six men for ten weeks, and all they've brought back is what amounts to a load of manure.' What had happened, he explained, was that the *Marbella* had struck a hurricane off the coast of Newfoundland. The ship had rolled so badly that the cargo of deep-frozen fish had broken the wooden boarding at the sides of the hold. Once the boarding had gone there had been nothing to protect the refrigeration pipes—either the wood or the frozen slabs of fish had fractured the pipe and there had been a burst.

'The stuff in the refrigeration pipes is tricoethylene, which is like dry-cleaning fluid. Of course it leaked, and contaminated the fish.' As a result, all the 220 tons of fish had been condemned. All Captain Downs could do now was arrange for the Ministry expert to see it, and agree that it should be sold for fishmeal to reduce the claim.

While Captain Downs was explaining, the fish were still coming out from the holds on the canvas conveyor, tucked in wallets like a cartridge belt. On the dockside the bobbers, as Hull fish porters are known, were loading them into crates. One of the frozen slabs fell on the ground and bounced as if it had been a cricket bat. Captain Downs picked it up—there must have been fifteen or twenty cod or pink bream frozen together in the slab, their eyes popping out like buttons.

'You can see that yellow stain along the side. That's been left by the tricoethylene.' Even in the icy air of the dockside, you could smell it.

Presently we went up on the deck and picked our way over the fishing gear. The way to the hold was down a long steel ladder. At the top one of the bobbers pushed back his red woollen cap and said I'd better borrow his gauntlets. 'You'll need to be careful where you put your feet down there.' I looked down closer into the hold. There must have still been fifty tons of fish, the slabs lying aslant each other like frozen see-saws.

'You can imagine what it was like down here in a Force Twelve.' The bobber who had lent me his gloves followed me down, shifting a slab of fish with the hook all bobbers carry, like some primitive surgical aid, because there is no other way of shifting fish. 'Catfish,' he said, looking it in the eye. 'That's a tasty fish.'

We slid precariously across the see-saws of fish to the side—in the refrigeration pipe there was a tiny gash, about the size of a fingernail. It was that which had caused the damage, said Captain Downs—that little nick in the pipe had cost the underwriters £40,000.

'At least there's one good thing,' said Captain Downs as we left. 'The crew are paid by contract. They won't lose by it.'

If the Lloyd's agent at Hull deals in anything from gum arabic to salami and Abyssinian rawhides, what about those in more exotic ports? Lloyd's has five hundred principal agents abroad, as well as another eight hundred sub-agents. In addition to intelligence and survey work, a foreign agent will also have to settle claims on behalf of the underwriter. Lloyd's world-wide reputation is such that any bank from Nice to Nicaragua will honour what is called a Lloyd's 'sight draft'. Issued by the agent on the spot, the draft, as its name implies, will be paid promptly to the insured person.

Lloyd's agents do not receive a salary. Like those at Hull, most work for Lloyd's as an incidental to their main business as general shipping agents. In most cases they are expected to provide the shipping intelligence free. Surveys and claims are paid for on a scale basis.

Beyond his run-of-the-mill work a Lloyd's agent will also be expected to provide the kind of political background material which could be of use to underwriters. 'It may be a port where some corrupt official is turning a blind eye to the fact that cargoes are being pushed into the sea, then claimed on,' says Mr Ronald Daly, Controller of Agencies. 'Or it may be a strike in South America which could affect contingency business. If an underwriter has to pay for delays, then it's in his interest to know if there might be a strike.' Information of this kind is noted in something about which Lloyd's tends to be reticent, the Pink Sheets, which go to all marine underwriters in the Room, as well as to outside subscribers, and are marked Confidential.

Sometimes an agent may find himself unexpectedly involved in police work. One day an Englishwoman who had been living in the West Indies came into the Intelligence Department to ask if they could help trace her husband who had gone off cruising in his yacht with another woman—somewhere, she thought, down the west coast of Africa. The Intelligence Department prides itself on always trying to help, even on the scantiest information. In the course of their enquiries they found that the husband was wanted by Interpol.

'It seemed they'd been looking for him for months,' says the Intelligence Department with modest pride, 'and we found him in two weeks. Once we knew the South African police were looking for him, we guessed he'd have made for South America. The closest point in South America to the African coast is a place called Fortaleza, so we sent a telegram to our agent there. He sent us back a reply immediately—both the yacht and the man were there.'

Another time the Devon police asked Lloyd's if they could trace a yacht called the *Angelique* that had been reported missing from Brixham. There was no sign of any vessel of that name in *Lloyd's List*, but one day somebody in the Intelligence Department noticed that another yacht, the *Astrolabe*, had just arrived at Corunna. It occurred to him that the first and last letters were the same, and that the number of letters between them fitted. So, when he looked it up, did the tonnage. The result was the arrest of the yacht-thieves within hours.

But perhaps the oddest story of a yacht recovery came when Mr O'Keefe, the Lloyd's agent at Bantry in Ireland, happened to notice a yacht called the *Lis* coming into the small – and as it turned out, aptly named – harbour of Crookhaven in Galway. Because the arrival of any new craft there was unusual, he went on board and met the owner. Meanwhile a local freelance photographer also took a picture of the *Lis*.

It appeared in a Cork newspaper, and also found its way to a London newspaper office. Here it happened to be seen by somebody who was interested in boats, and who remembered having read about a yacht called the *Melisse* which had been stolen from the Hamble River near Southampton. He got in touch with

Lloyd's, who instructed Mr O'Keefe to return to Crookhaven. Closer inspection by the somewhat embarrassed Lloyd's agent showed that the name had been painted out except for the three central letters. In the end it was those three letters which led to the yacht's recovery.

At Lloyd's everything comes back to the Room. And if there is one image of Lloyd's more evocative than anything else, it is the sight of underwriters' clerks copying down their notes from the Casualty Boards. It is the point where the world of business meets the sea, the world of rusty coasters and kerosene drums and Force Nine gales. It is where an excess-of-loss policy has something to do with four drowned sailors on a life-raft.

The news posted on the Casualty Boards may be anything from the loss of a jet airliner to a small fire in a coaster's hold—if it is a casualty, it will go on the Board. The notice itself will be written, by tradition, in longhand on a foolscap sheet—yellow for marine casualties, pink for non-marine and blue for aviation. Three times an hour a waiter from the Intelligence Department collects the casualty sheets, goes over to the Room and posts them on the Board.

Only one member of the Intelligence Department actually works in the Room. This is the clerk who has the job – almost as time-honoured as the Caller's – of writing in that most legendary volume of Lloyd's, the Loss Book. Sitting at a desk in the centre of the Room, he has to make the often difficult decision as to when a casualty has become a loss. 'If a ship has clearly gone down,' explained Geoffrey Luben, the present Loss Book Clerk, 'then there isn't a problem. Where I do have to make a decision is where a ship may have suffered serious damage, but isn't a total loss—the sort of situation where a tanker may get a bad fire in her hold.'

Although its early volumes are among the treasures of Lloyd's, Mr Luben explained that the Loss Book on its lectern is not simply a picturesque survival. The point of putting a loss in the Book is that the underwriters may have it brought to their attention.

'The clerks,' he says, 'will see me writing, then come over to see the name of the ship that's lost. They'll copy down details of what I've put in the Book—then go back to their boxes and look up their records to see if they've got a line on the ship concerned. If the underwriter has got a big line, he may want to go on the overdue market and lay it off with reinsurance. If it's a sinking, there's nothing he can do about it.'

Besides actually writing in the Book, the Clerk's job is to gather information for the Intelligence Department from the Room. If there is an overdue, the brokers may have been given news by the owner, and it is part of the Loss Book Clerk's experience that he will know which brokers to ask.

What, I asked Mr Luben, about the Lutine Bell? Didn't recording a casualty also involve the sounding of Lloyd's most historic symbol?

Nowadays, he said rather regretfully, it didn't. Most people supposed the bell was rung every time there was a loss, but this no longer happened. On the rare occasions when the Bell is still sounded, its purpose is to stop dealings in the overdue market. This means that when a vessel is overdue, Mr Luben's job is to find out at what reinsurance rate it is being written in the Room. The fears for the ship will be reflected in the amount of premium which the underwriter has to pay to reduce his commitment.

If the rate goes beyond a certain point, then Lloyd's rule is that the Bell must be rung as soon as there is news of the ship; if the news is given to the whole market at once, then no underwriter can have the advantage of special knowledge (as, for instance, Samuel Pepys had over the vessel described on page 16. One marine underwriter pointed out to me that this was a good example of the kind of thing the ringing of the Bell is designed to prevent).

With modern communications the need seldom, in any case,

arises. Mr Luben told me the Bell had only been rung once for an overdue in the three years he had worked as Intelligence Clerk in the Room. That had been for a ship called the *Venus Challenger* which had been overdue during the Indo-Pakistan war in 1972. The market had written a lot of reinsurance on her, before she had been found sunk twenty-six miles from Karachi.

Presently Mr Luben said it was time for him to draw the line—at four-thirty every afternoon he gets out one of the traditional quill pens and rules a red line under the day's losses. Until recently Lloyd's used goose-quills for the Loss Book, but he prefers the swan-quills, which come from the Swannery at Abbotsbury in Dorset. The actual writing is done with the point of the quill, which has been cut after being hardened in hot sand—'not too hot, or it'll split when you start writing'.

A good quill, he explained, would last about a fortnight. Most are made nowadays by a seventeen-year-old boy from Yeovil, so the craft seems safe for some years to come. Mr Luben himself learnt his calligraphy from writing the ordinary notices for the Casualty Boards. Writing with a quill, he told me, is more difficult but it gives the writing a sharpness. 'All the visitors to Lloyd's come to see the Loss Book, and I feel the writing should be of the best.'

The Intelligence Clerk in the Room has one other daily task, and it is among Lloyd's more endearing aspects. Every day he writes perhaps thirty postcards to the wives of ships' captains who have asked to be told the movements of their husband's ships. Sometimes a captain's wife will receive as many as three postcards a week to tell her for what port her husband is bound, and his expected date of arrival.

The service is provided free to captain's wives; theoretically other wives are supposed to pay 50p for fifty postcards, but Mr Luben reckons he sends another twenty-five a week of these, and doesn't recall the Department ever sending a bill in. 'Usually,' he says, 'they write and thank us when the ships come home. It's the sort of thing we like to do at Lloyd's.'

Such human services aside, Lloyd's main channel to the world is through its publications. Pre-eminent among these is *Lloyd's List*; the oldest daily newspaper in the world, it has an unbroken record of publication since 1734. Today it consists of about fourteen pages of which the second half is entirely given up to shipping information. Underwriters receive *Lloyd's List* by subscription, though most of its 11,000 circulation comes from people outside. For instance, if a wholesale fruiterer in Manchester is expecting a load of oranges from Cyprus he can find out from the 'Ships Expected' page what port the ship is due to dock at.

In addition to the detailed information of maritime movements, *Lloyd's List* also contains several pages of news likely to be of interest to the shipping and insurance markets. Headlines can be anything from news of a launch or a new cargo terminus in New York to developments about the Channel Tunnel. 'Our readers,' says Mr Jack Prince, the editor, 'aren't interested in whether a new P & O liner has pink bathrooms. What they do want to know is whether she's got the latest electronic devices on the bridge.'

Apart from reporting visits of touring celebrities to Lloyd's, there is little of what could be called chat, and no general news except where it touches shipping or insurance. 'If the Prime Minister was assassinated,' says Mr Prince, 'it wouldn't make the lead. We'd give it a mention—but basically our job is to cover stories that other people wouldn't.'

Still more specialized is Lloyd's other daily publication, the *Shipping Index*. A fat volume giving as many as 18,000 separate shipping movements, it is required reading for coastguards, harbour masters and almost anyone concerned with the sea. Apart from these, the Department also publishes a *Casualty Index*, its own law reports, and the most comprehensive series of maritime atlases in the world. But from the underwriter's point of view, probably the most useful of the Department's ten publications is one it does not officially admit to at all. This is the 1,000-page *Confidential Index of Shipping*,* issued twice a year to subscribers only.

When I went to see Ken Mason, Lloyd's Shipping Editor, he explained that while other shipping lists give details of tonnage and nominal owners, it is only in the *Confidential Index* that you could see who was the real owner of each ship. Nowadays, for tax reasons, a lot of ship-owners register each vessel as a separate company, rather than listing them all in one fleet. Mr Mason said it was something that a lot of Continental ship-owners did, and it didn't make life easier for the underwriter, because there might be some ship-owners he wasn't too keen on insuring.

'If a broker asks him to write a risk on a ship,' he explained, 'he can see at a glance from the *Confidential Index* if she's what we call a one-off—that is if she's registered as a one-ship company. Then he can turn back to see who owns the one-off. If it's someone he's not too happy about, he won't write the risk.'

Besides listing ship-owners' fleets, the *Confidential Index* also adds a casualty list of previous losses suffered by the owner. 'It may be a bit like reading out a man's police record in court,' says Mr Mason, 'but in this case we're here to help the underwriter.' Another point included will be the year the ship was built. In the case of a ship more than fifteen years old the underwriter will very likely want a higher premium.

Did many ship-owners resent the details of their fleets being exposed to the public gaze like this? Mr Mason said on the whole he thought they didn't. He sends all ship-owners the proofs relating to their ships, and three-quarters of the owners send them back corrected. There had only been one time, he said, when he had thought they had made a serious mistake over a

* *Lloyd's Register of Shipping*, the underwriter's other required reading, is published by an entirely separate organization, though Lloyd's representatives sit on the Board. It is the *Register* which includes classification of ships, among them the famous 'A1 at Lloyd's'.

ship's age. That had been when an Italian ship-owner had written to complain that the *Confidential Index* showed one of his vessels as having been built in 1940 when in fact she had been built in 1948. 'He enclosed documents to prove it,' says Mr Mason, 'and this time I really thought we had boobed.'

When Lloyd's got to work on looking up the details, they uncovered an extraordinary story. The ship had been built in Holland in 1940. Her keel had been laid in May, at the time of the German occupation, and the German fleet had taken her over. She had sailed under the Swastika for three years, then hit a mine off Denmark in 1944. She sank in the Kattegat, breaking in two pieces. After the war she was raised from the bottom, taken back to Hamburg, and repaired. Finally, in 1948, she had emerged from her long ordeal and been sold as a new ship to her present owner.

'I had to tell him that she'd not only been sailing all that time,' says Ken Mason. 'What he didn't know was that his ship had spent four years lying in two halves on the bottom of the bloody ocean.'

The world loves a story of courage: consider that of Captain Christoforos Kakkaris, master of the tanker *Kymo*. On a winter afternoon in 1972 the *Kymo* was bound from the East Indies to Japan with a cargo of resin and fuel oil, when there was an explosion amidships which set fire to the bridge and the officers' quarters.

Within ten minutes the crew were safely away in the boats, but not Captain Kakkaris. He jumped from the blazing bridge, managed to drop the port anchor, then tried to get through the blazing afterpart. Because of the fire he could not reach it, so he dived overboard and swam back to the stern. With the help of the Chief Engineer and three crew members, he fought the fire and brought it under control, three times refusing to leave his ship.

Some months later Captain Kakkaris received a unique

reward for his courage. It was announced that, as well as a cash award, he was to be given Lloyd's Silver Medal which is only given for extreme heroism at sea. The other crew members who had helped him were also awarded medals. In making the award to Captain Kakkaris, the Committee were carrying on one of their oldest traditions—the idea that because Lloyd's insures ships, it has an obligation to those who risk their lives in them.

The first tangible expression of this sense of obligation goes back to 1782 when the members of Lloyd's raised £2,000 for the dependants of seamen lost in the *Royal George*. Possibly *The Times* overstated the case a little when it described the Committee of Lloyd's as 'the father of every seaman's orphan'. Even so, in those days when there was no kind of state help for those disabled in war or for their dependants, it was a beginning.

It was not until the Napoleonic Wars that Lloyd's charitable effort began in earnest. In 1794, after the Glorious First of June, a series of funds was begun to help those wounded in particular battles. The fund for the Glorious First of June raised £21,000. Then, in 1798, came the Battle of the Nile. It was a victory which touched Lloyd's underwriters' pockets as well as their patriotism. Because of it, British merchantmen could now sail unmolested through the Mediterranean.

The members of Lloyd's showed their gratitude to the tune of nearly £40,000. All sailors who lost a leg or an arm in the battle got £40. Nelson himself, we might feel a little disproportionately, was voted £500 to buy a silver dinner service, which he duly ordered from Rundall & Bridge, the City silversmiths.

Although there is no actual record of the presentation, it seems likely it took place on 15 November 1801, when he was reported in *The Times* as 'having been upon the Royal Exchange some time'. Six months later, after the Copenhagen fund was raised, he seems to have planned to visit Lloyd's again, for he wrote to Angerstein: 'I feel – and I am certain every Officer and man in the Fleet does the same – much indebted to the Gentlemen of the Committee for the attention they pay, and trouble they experience, on this occasion. I hope in a few days to have it in my power to pay my respects personally to them.'

Meanwhile the more general fund-raising was still going on, and in 1803 a Meeting of Lloyd's Subscribers was held to inaugurate what was to be called the Patriotic Fund. This was to be a campaign on a national scale, based on Lloyd's as today such fund-raising is based on the Mansion House. Like the previous Lloyd's funds, its objects were to help the wounded and their dependants, or as the Committee rather dramatically put it:

> To animate the efforts of our Defenders by Sea and Land, . . . for the purpose of assuaging the anguish of their Wounds, or palliating in some degree the more weighty misfortune of the loss of Limbs – of alleviating the Distresses of the Widow and Orphan – of soothing the brow of Sorrow for the fall of their dearest Relatives, the props of unhappy Indigence or helpless Age . . . the Mite of the Labourer combining with the Munificent Donation of the Noble and Wealthy shall be the best pledge of our Unanimity.

The Committee's prose style may have been a little carried away, but there was no doubt of the campaign's success. The City companies and other insurance offices contributed their thousands and the Labourers, as the Committee had hopefully anticipated, their Mites. Three watermen of Shadwell Docks sent £5. Theatres gave the proceeds of special performances; the Bank of England and the East India Company gave £5,000 each.

Apart from the more general charitable purposes, much of the money went, as before, on presentations. After Trafalgar the recipients included all Nelson's captains, who were each given a silver cup designed by Flaxman. Lady Nelson was given plate, and so was Commodore Dance, who had beaten off a French squadron with his fleet of East Indiamen.

Curiously, it does not seem to have occurred to the

Committee of Lloyd's that it might be a shade presumptuous to set up what was really a sort of private Honours List. Probably they did not take much notice of the radical journalist William Cobbett, who objected to what he called 'a set of traders at Lloyd's' usurping the function of the Crown by awarding honours. But when they presented a silver vase to Sir Home Popham for his expedition to Buenos Aires, it was too much even for the Admiralty. Popham's adventure had turned out a disaster and he was court-martialled. The First Lord described the Patriotic Fund as 'that mischievous system of awards administered by the Committee of Lloyd's'. In 1809, ostensibly at least because of the calls on the Fund arising from the heavy casualty lists in the Peninsular War, the presentations were tactfully abandoned.

Over the years a good deal of the great dinner service presented to Nelson has been bought back. Today it forms the centrepiece of what is known as the Nelson Room at Lloyd's. In it you may see Nelson's Order of the Bath, various letters to Angerstein and the Log Book of the *Euryalus*, which as the signal-repeating frigate at Trafalgar recorded Nelson's most famous signal during the battle. As to the dinner service itself, it has been kept lovingly through the years, not least by Nelson himself who often referred to it with pride, and had a special sea-chest made to take it. Since its return to Lloyd's it has only been once used—at a dinner given by the Committee in 1948 to honour Sir Winston Churchill.

Meanwhile there have been many less ostentatious ways, over the centuries, in which Lloyd's has shown its sense of obligation. One of the outstanding instances was the help it gave to Henry Greathead, who is often credited with the invention of the lifeboat. The story is so odd, adventurous and inextricably linked with Lloyd's that it is worth telling in a little detail.

Wind-swept and sea-fretted, the small grey town of South Shields lies on the Durham bank of the Tyne, guarded by a traditionally perilous group of rocks called the Black Middens.

It is known as a clannish place. The craft of pilotage in the harbour entry is still handed down from father to son. 'Arl tiggither like the folks of Shields' has long been the popular saying. Even today there is a hint that somebody from Newcastle or Darlington is a little foreign.

The clannishness may be one reason why South Shields people have only a grudging pride in Henry Greathead. Originally born at Richmond in Yorkshire, he came to Shields as a boy and learned his trade there as a ship's carpenter. In 1779 he was on a ship bound from the Tyne to Grenada. A few days out of port, he discovered that the ship's master planned to wreck her on the Goodwins to get the insurance money. With the aid of some of the rest of the crew, Greathead managed to prevent the captain's design, but could not stop him running the ship aground off Calais later. The captain then went to the port authorities at Calais, swore an affidavit that the ship had gone aground because of bad weather, and called his crew to sign it with him.

Greathead not only refused to sign the affidavit, but got several of the rest of the crew members to refuse as well. On his return to London he went to Lloyd's and told them the true story. He met several of the underwriters, among them one named James Forsyth, and another named Peter Warren who was a partner of Angerstein's. Thanks to the information he gave, they were able to refuse the owner's claim.

All this was the mere prologue to Greathead's later adventures. From now on his experiences read like something in a boy's adventure story. He was captured by American privateers in the Caribbean, offered a commission in the American Navy, and twice press-ganged by the British. Continuing to behave like a hero of fiction, he returned home in 1783 to South Shields to marry the humble girl he had always loved. But Greathead had one other ambition.

All his life – and after his adventures no one could have been more aware of the need – he had been working on a plan for what he called a safety-boat or life-boat. He got back to Shields, settled to a boat-building business, and in his spare time began work on the life-boat.

Before long, however, he became faced with that perennial problem for inventors, a shortage of cash. He began to think around the problem and remembered Lloyd's. Now that he needed help to complete his designs, who better to approach than the underwriters he had himself helped, four years earlier? He wrote to Forsyth and Warren, enclosing his drawings. True to the storybook pattern of Greathead's life, the Lloyd's underwriters did not merely write back praising Greathead's designs; they sent money, and an introduction to the Duke of Northumberland, who visited Greathead's workshop.

It is at this point that the fictional element ends in Greathead's life and a more human note of conflict enters. Curiously there was another local man working on the idea of a life-boat – or perhaps it is not so curious if you stand even today on Beacon Hill at Shields, listening to the gong-like sounds of the buoys, looking out to the Black Middens from the site where the local people used to light beacons to guide in shipwrecked sailors.

The name of the rival inventor was the unlikely one of Willie Wouldhave, and he was in every way Greathead's opposite. As Greathead was clearly urbane, practical and efficient, so Wouldhave seems to have been sour, eccentric and possessed of an explosive temper. Born in Liddle Street, North Shields, in 1751, he had turned his hand to building clocks, electrical apparatus and organs as well as life-boats. Almost the archetypal figure of the inventor, his pictures show him as having the harrowed, elongated features of an El Greco portrait.

When Wouldhave began work on designing a life-boat is not clear, but one local legend of him is not unworthy of comparison with the insight of a Fleming or a Newton. One day, it is said, he went to the local well to get a drink. There was a woman drawing water at the well, and she asked him to help her with her skeel—the traditional local name for a pail of water.

Floating in the water in her skeel was a piece of a broken wooden dish or scoop—presumably it was something like the shape of a slice of melon, for Wouldhave noticed that it floated with the points upward. However it was dropped in the water, it righted itself. Wouldhave went home, and from that day began to think in terms of a design which would right itself, as the piece of broken scoop had done, in the roughest water.

Meanwhile, in the late 1780s, there had been a long chain of shipwrecks off South Shields. These had reached their climax in the wreck, in September 1789, of a ship called the *Adventure* which had gone aground with heavy loss of life. Public opinion in South Shields had been so appalled by this succession of disasters that it was decided to hold a competition for a life-boat. A committee was formed by a local society called the Gentlemen of the Lawe-House. Somewhere in the latter end of 1789 it met to consider the rival designs, under the chairmanship of one Nicholas Fairless.

How many other designs there were besides those of Greathead and Wouldhave we do not know—but we do know that they both entered. Greathead's was long and flat, with no buoyancy from cork or airboxes.

Wouldhave's, by contrast, had a high prow and stern, like the piece of broken scoop he had seen floating in the woman's skeel. At both ends there were watertight cases containing cork for extra buoyancy, and there was more cork along the floor. The model itself was twenty-two feet long and made of tin. Its other feature was that it had what boat-builders call a sheer—a cutaway, slanting shape to the sides of the hull.

Whatever the committee thought of the models, the personal impression made by Wouldhave was disastrous. Asked by Nicholas Fairless what advantage it had over its rivals, Wouldhave is said to have turned angrily upon him. 'Why, I say it will neither sink nor go to pieces nor lie bottom up. Will any of yours do as much?'

Perhaps it was a question the committee did not care to answer. They decided that neither design was suitable, but that Wouldhave should be awarded one guinea by way of compensation for his efforts. Even in those days the prize must have seemed derisory, and Wouldhave refused it with contempt.

What could the Gentlemen of the Lawe-House do now? In the manner of committees, they decided on a compromise. It was arranged that Fairless and the more amenable Greathead should combine their efforts—Fairless presumably merely holding a watching brief on behalf of the committee. But the design they should work on would incorporate Wouldhave's essential features of the high prow and stern, as well as the cork for buoyancy.

Greathead and Fairless must have worked fast. Between the loss of the *Adventure* which had inspired the competition and the actual launching, there was a period of only four months. First Greathead made a clay model. It was like Wouldhave's tin one, but it contained the important new feature of having a cambered keel instead of a straight one. The model was inspected and approved, and Greathead was commissioned to build the boat at a cost of £91.

Thirty feet long and built to carry a crew of ten, she was launched on 31 January 1790, and named, perhaps a little ambiguously, the *Original.* The date of her first rescue is obscure, but evidently proved the life-boat's worth. It was of seven men who were rescued from the sloop *Edinburgh* in a sea 'so monstrous that no other boat could have lived in it'.

Over the next twelve years Greathead's boatyard appears to have flourished. He built twenty-one life-boats, including one to the Duke of Northumberland's order for the neighbouring seaport town of North Shields. His own fame began to spread and was even celebrated in verse, as in the 'Ode addressed to Mr Greathead the Inventor by Dr Trotter, Physician to the Fleet':

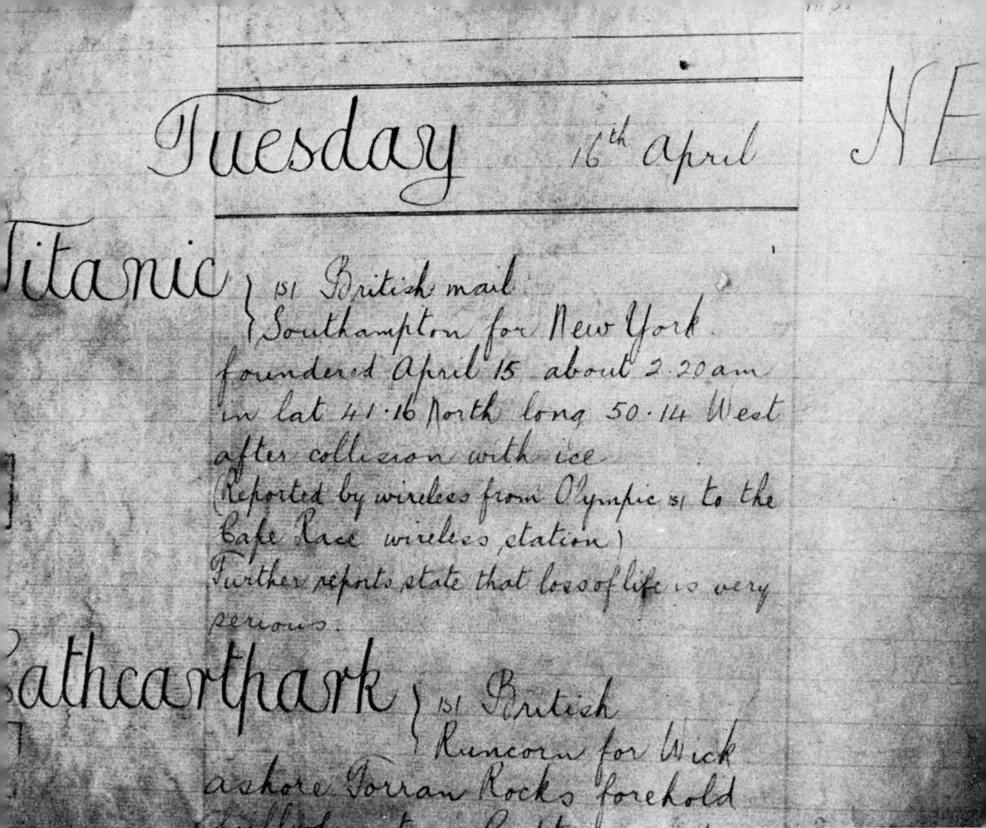
Tuesday 16th April

Titanic } SS British mail
Southampton for New York
foundered April 15 about 2.20 am
in lat 41.16 North long 50.14 West
after collision with ice
(Reported by wireless from Olympic SS to the
Cape Race wireless station)
Further reports state that loss of life is very
serious.

Cathcartpark } SS British
Runcorn for Wick
ashore Torran Rocks forehold

16

The *Titanic* entry in the loss book with, *below*, part of the slip. The figures represent each underwriter's 'line', with his initials next to it.

17

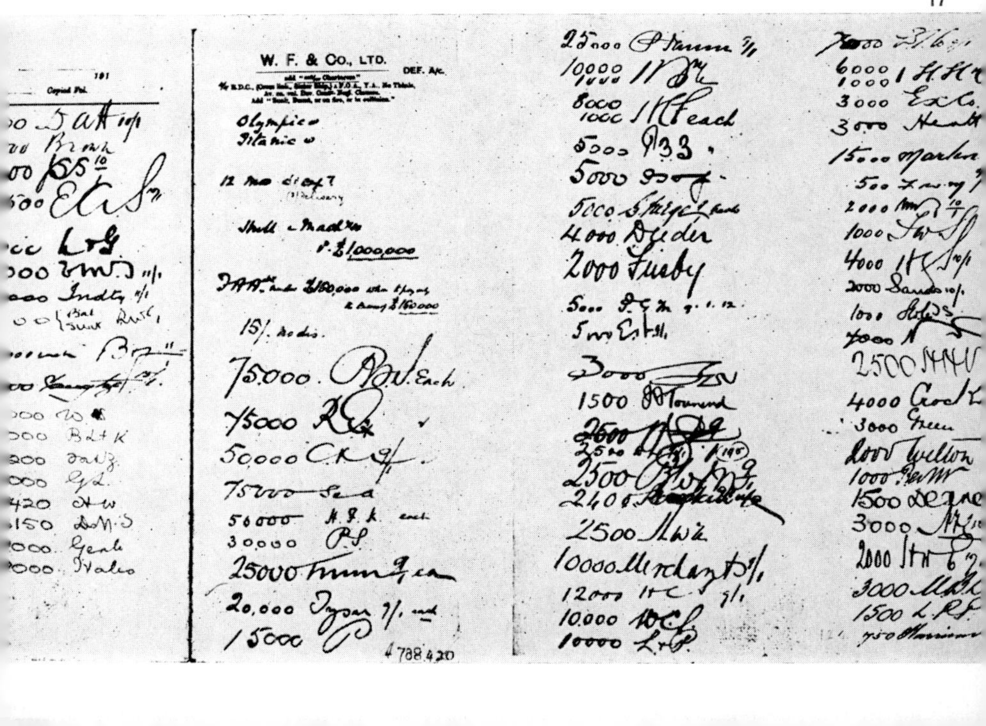
W. F. & Co., LTD.
DEF. A/c.

18

Lloyd's reputation in America grew when underwriters paid up promptly on the claims arising from the 1906 San Francisco earthquake and fire (*above*). One of the market's heaviest losses in recent years resulted from the devastation caused by Hurricane Betsy in 1965 (*below*).

19

20

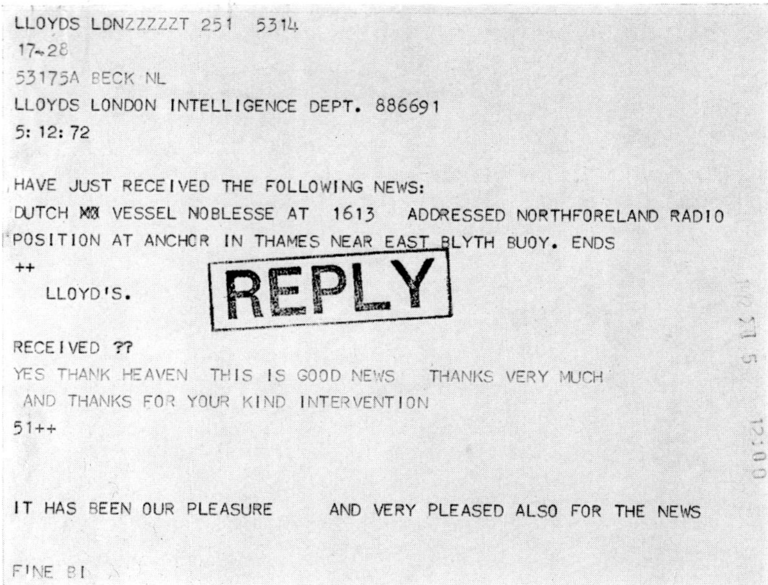
LLOYDS LDNZZZZZT 251 5314
17-28
53175A BECK NL
LLOYDS LONDON INTELLIGENCE DEPT. 886691
5: 12: 72

HAVE JUST RECEIVED THE FOLLOWING NEWS:
DUTCH XX VESSEL NOBLESSE AT 1613 ADDRESSED NORTHFORELAND RADIO
POSITION AT ANCHOR IN THAMES NEAR EAST BLYTH BUOY. ENDS
++
LLOYD'S.

REPLY

RECEIVED ??
YES THANK HEAVEN THIS IS GOOD NEWS THANKS VERY MUCH
AND THANKS FOR YOUR KIND INTERVENTION
51++

IT HAS BEEN OUR PLEASURE AND VERY PLEASED ALSO FOR THE NEWS

FINE BI

Lloyd's Intelligence Department is a vital source of world shipping information. This exchange of telex messages let her Dutch owners know that the *Noblesse* was safe (see page 125).

A Lloyd's agent in every part. View from the office of the Rotterdam agent.

21

22 23

The Casualty Board (*left*). 'The yellow, pink and blue notices announce the day's consignment of destruction.' *Right* and *below*, activity at one of the underwriters' boxes.

24

25

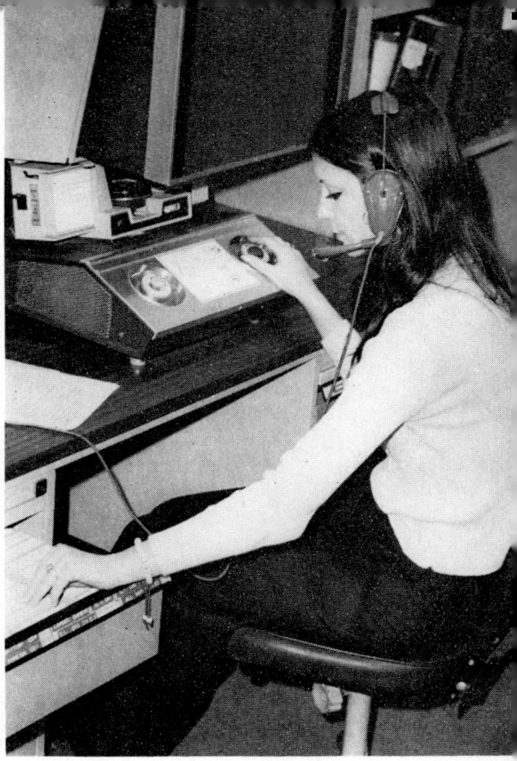

26

e marine market occupies the und floor. The gallery upstairs ıses the non-marine market and ıdentally provides a handy vantage point for visitors.

Microfilming the *Confidential Index*. Lloyd's was one of the first City organizations to use computers.

The slip for the Loch Ness Monster. 'In the event of loss hereunder the Monster shall become the property of underwriters hereon.' Note the syndicate stamps on the right of the slip—even in the non-marine market the symbol of an anchor is still used.

27

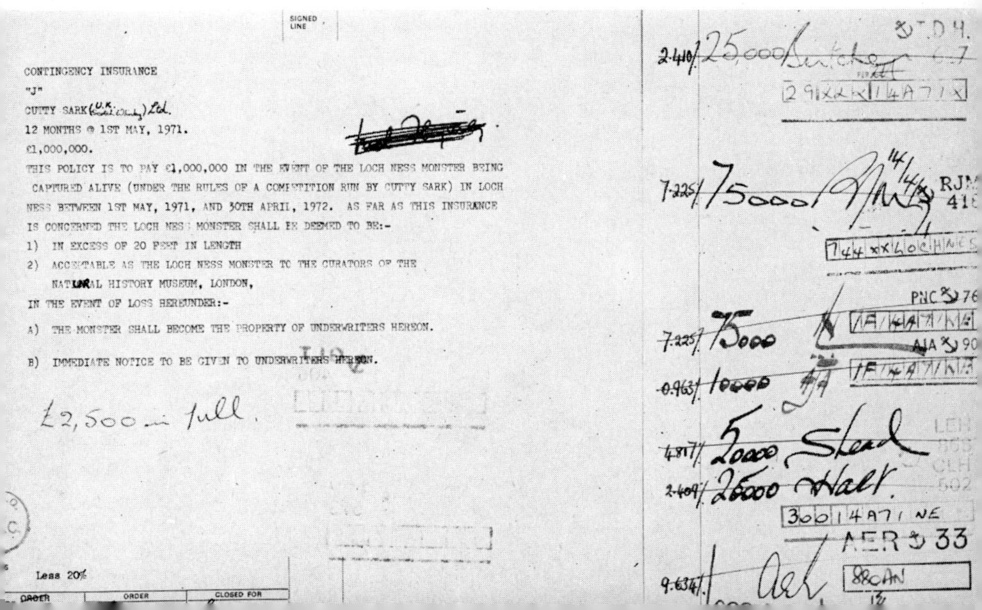

SIGNED LINE

CONTINGENCY INSURANCE

"J"

CUTTY SARK (U.K. ...) Ltd.

12 MONTHS @ 1ST MAY, 1971.

£1,000,000.

THIS POLICY IS TO PAY £1,000,000 IN THE EVENT OF THE LOCH NESS MONSTER BEING CAPTURED ALIVE (UNDER THE RULES OF A COMPETITION RUN BY CUTTY SARK) IN LOCH NESS BETWEEN 1ST MAY, 1971, AND 30TH APRIL, 1972. AS FAR AS THIS INSURANCE IS CONCERNED THE LOCH NESS MONSTER SHALL BE DEEMED TO BE:-

1) IN EXCESS OF 20 FEET IN LENGTH

2) ACCEPTABLE AS THE LOCH NESS MONSTER TO THE CURATORS OF THE NATURAL HISTORY MUSEUM, LONDON,

IN THE EVENT OF LOSS HEREUNDER:-

A) THE MONSTER SHALL BECOME THE PROPERTY OF UNDERWRITERS HEREON.

B) IMMEDIATE NOTICE TO BE GIVEN TO UNDERWRITERS HEREON.

£2,500 in full.

Less 20%

ORDER | ORDER | CLOSED FOR

2.410/ 25,000

7.225/ 75000

RJM 41

PNC 76

7.225/ 75000

AIA 90

0.963/ 10000

4.817/ 20000 Stead

2.409/ 25000 Hall.

AER 33

9.634/

Innovation is one c
Lloyd's stronges
traditions. Today
underwriters have t
be experts on every
thing from large non
marine risks, such a
the new Londo
Bridge, to North Se
oil rigs.

30

One of the problems of modern insurance is the huge size of risk. Today a tanker or container ship carries a cargo that not long ago would have been divided among several ships.

31

32
'Of all the Perils and Adventures listed in the Lloyd's policy of 1779 there is still one th is a terrifying word to any seaman and that is "fire".' The former *Queen Elizabe* (*above*) still lies partly submerged in Hong Kong harbour after the fire which swept h during her conversion into a floating university in 1972.

Hijacking is an increasing risk for the aviation insurer. Arab terrorists blew up thr international airliners at Dawson's Field in 1970 (*below*).
33

'A gift beyond the poet's flame,
A grateful crew shall incense burn,
And GREATHEAD shine in deathless fame,
While love and friendship hail the tar's return!'

Even so, there was an unending need for funds. When Greathead appealed to the House of Commons in 1801, the House was too involved with the Napoleonic Wars to spend money on life-boats. It was left to Lloyd's, in the following year, to make far the largest contribution that had yet been made to the life-boat service. On 20 May 1802, on Angerstein's initiative, the underwriters of Lloyd's voted £2,000 'for the encouragement of life-boats being instituted in different parts of the coast of this kingdom'. The immediate result was the building of fourteen life-boats for coastal towns from Lowestoft to Fishguard and Newhaven to Arbroath. The more far-reaching result was the setting up, in 1824, of the National Life-boat Institution, the forerunner of the present RNLI.

Meanwhile in South Shields they still argue about who actually invented the life-boat. Wouldhave died in poverty in 1821 and was buried in the churchyard of St Hilda's, the stone eighteenth-century church which dominates the town and looks towards the Bergen and Oslo quays. Today a stone commemorates him as the inventor of 'that blessing to mankind, the life-boat'. Certainly much of the evidence seems to support the claim. Even apart from the story of the skeel, there is something dark and flickering in what we know of his character that suggests the true inventor.

On the other hand an idea is often produced as much by a climate of inventive thought as by an individual; perhaps a truer perspective would show Wouldhave as the lonely genius, but Greathead as the practical man who, seeing the importance of actually getting the life-boat built, had the good sense not to offend the committee that proposed to build it.

Ultimately any great project needs both aspects, and both are commemorated on a single monument that stands today near the seafront at South Shields. Built in 1890, it bears the names and carved faces of both men. Next to it stands their true memorial—the South Shields life-boat *Tyne*, which between 1833 and 1890 saved over 1,000 lives.

Today Lloyd's co-operates on legislation for greater safety at sea with world-wide organizations ranging from the Admiralty and the US Coast Guard to IMCO, the Inter-Governmental Maritime Consultative Organization. One recent example of Lloyd's co-operation with IMCO was the revision of the safety rules for trans-Atlantic yachtsmen, who had become worried because the old signal MIK – 'Report me to Lloyd's' – had been abandoned.

With the universal use of radio, the signal had been thought to be no longer needed. But what would happen, the yachtsmen asked, if the radio broke down and there was no means of reporting their position to passing ships? Mr Tom Hill of Lloyd's Intelligence Department took the yachtsmen's case to an international conference, which submitted the proposed change in regulations to IMCO. From 1974 onwards the famous signal 'Report me to Lloyd's' goes back in the book of signals.

Today, as always through its three hundred years of history, Lloyd's means ships. 'We are all obliged by your humane attention to us seamen,' wrote Nelson to Angerstein once, identifying himself as always with the humblest.

Today, though it may take different forms, the attention to seamen is still there. It may be a weekly postcard to a captain's wife, or it may be the total resources of the Intelligence Deparment brought into play to help a vessel in danger. It may be a medal for a Greek sailor, or hours of time-consuming research to give pleasure to some small boy or old sailor who writes in to ask if Lloyd's can help him identify a ship.

In the end it is the quality which sets Lloyd's apart—the extra dimension of service.

8
All Risks

ONE day in 1967 Lloyd's underwriters emerging from the Room at lunchtime saw a bit of excitement—a convoy of armoured cars with a police escort heading up Leadenhall Street towards the Bank of England with £63 million worth of bullion. For the good of their digestions it is perhaps as well that they did not know they had themselves insured it. Each of the five armoured cars was covered at Lloyd's for £15 million, but the market knew nothing about it.

The background to the incident is among the more remarkable examples of Lloyd's sense of trust. Several weeks earlier the Bank of England's broker had approached Mr Robert Gordon, a Lloyd's underwriter who specializes in insuring valuables in transit. A large amount of bullion was to be flown from Fort Knox to Mildenhall aerodrome in Suffolk; the Bank wanted to insure it while it was being taken from the airfield to their vaults. There was only one stipulation, which for any ordinary insurance company would have made it unthinkable. Both for political and security reasons, nobody was to know the gold was being moved, or was even present in Britain.

Mr Gordon considered the matter. He knew there was a twelve-months contract in existence for normal sendings and decided it was the sort of situation where Lloyd's both could and ought to help. He mentioned it to one other underwriter, without telling him the subject of the risk or where it was going. The other man agreed that Gordon should accept it on behalf of the underwriters concerned. 'If there had been a loss,' says Gordon, 'I believe the market would have backed my judgement and paid up.' When the Room finally got to hear of what had happened, nobody complained that Gordon's judgement had been wrong.

Since then, machinery has been set up whereby Lloyd's marine market can insure any such exceptional risk without being told the details. The method was used in 1972 when one of the world's most famous diamonds was taken from New York to London. The slip contained a clause saying simply that all security should be agreed by the leading underwriter. Lloyd's underwriters had a risk on it of nearly a million pounds, but do not know to this day how the diamond travelled. Nor are they likely to. Robert Gordon fends off all probing questions with a bland smile and the observation that he might need to use the method again.

How does a Lloyd's underwriter come to get involved in the world of top security? Mr Gordon is in his early fifties, slim and rather stylishly dressed, with a quiet line in the sort of deadpan humour which is popular in the Room. Despite his youthful look, he is a grandfather, and lives with his large and cheerfully extrovert family in a small country house at Great Wakering, just outside Southend. As an underwriter for the C. I. de Rougemont syndicate, he writes for around eighty names. De Rougemont's is one of the oldest syndicates in Lloyd's and is independent of any broker. Although only a small part of his business is insuring ships, his box is technically in the marine market. 'The link really began in the nineteenth century,' he says, 'when the syndicate began insuring gold in sailing ships going to the Far East. Today it may be Eurobonds, works of art or platinum catalysts for the oil industry. If it's valuable, we'll write it.'

To see how the complex business of writing such insurance works, Mr Gordon suggested I might like to sit on his box for a bit. When I got there, there was a young broker with what Mr Gordon said was rather an unusual slip. There was going to be an exhibition of modern painting at the Orangerie in Paris, and a collector who was lending fifteen paintings by Derain wanted the Gallery to pay the insurance cover.

'The thing is, he wants the Gallery to insure them for a total loss,' said the broker. The phrase sounded a touch maritime for modern paintings. 'Even in the case of minor damage. If there's the slightest scratch on one of them, we'd have to pay the full value.'

Mr Gordon nodded and said the client seemed to be a bit perfectionist. 'Suppose you had a picture of a girl's face by a tree, and you get the beginning of a scratch on the face, but most of it on the tree. I'm thinking of something like that, a small scratch or a pinprick. Are they going to be exhibited behind glass?'

'I think you could make it a condition.' The broker watched while Mr Gordon wrote 'to be exhibited out of public reach', then transposed one of the clauses so that it said major damage would be assessed by an outside expert, not by the assured himself.

The broker moved on; next was another young man who asked if Mr Gordon would care to write some catastrophe cover in Venezuela.

'It wouldn't do for me,' said Mr Gordon courteously. 'I don't write earthquakes.'

The broker said helpfully that he could call it wind if Mr Gordon liked, but there was nothing doing. Meanwhile his deputy was looking up something in a book—another broker wanted to know if the de Rougemont box could tell him whether a particular jeweller was all right. The jeweller in question did not appear to figure in the book. The broker went off, and the deputy underwriter put the book back. 'It's what we call our Shady File,' he said. 'If someone's had a claim we don't like the look of, we put their names in red.'

Meanwhile another broker had come up with a slip about someone taking some Ming vases from Milan to Sydney. They were to go in the care of a friend of the client, but Mr Gordon looked doubtful. He might write them ex-fidelity, which meant excluding the possibility that the friend ran off with them. Even so he'd want to know who had valued them.

'They'd have to be kept in this man's care in the cabin. I'd want them warranted in his sight or hand at all times.'

The broker said what happened if the man wanted to go to the toilet—it was a long way from Milan to Sydney. Mr Gordon said he wasn't worried about that, but there was something he didn't like about the whole thing. 'I don't know why, but it smells.'

Afterwards I asked him why, and he told me it was something you couldn't define, but there had been rather a lot of cases of fraud lately where valuables were being carried by friends. 'Once you have a pattern of something you begin to get suspicious. It rings an alarm. Once it's done that, you can't get rid of the idea there's something wrong.'

When he started underwriting, Mr Gordon said, there had been very little security-consciousness at Lloyd's. In the late 1950s he had suggested that the market should take security precautions as a natural extension of the risks it wrote. He was told that if Lloyd's was to initiate loss prevention methods, the premiums would be reduced. 'The general view was "Let's have more premiums and risk the losses". Within three years it was becoming apparent that this didn't work. We were having to put up the premiums to a point where people wouldn't be able to stay in business if they paid them.'

Since then security-consciousness has grown in the Room. Gordon himself sits on a Home Office Crime Prevention Committee as a representative of Lloyd's. The marine market has also appointed its own security man, an ex-Scotland Yard officer named Commander Gerrard, whose work ranges from checking on everything from art galleries to banks and airports. When one famous painting was taken to its unidentified port of departure from the gallery, the Commander carried it down Bond Street, wrapped in a piece of sack. 'It seemed,' says Gordon, 'the way to attract least attention.'

Another time Gordon's caution not only saved himself and other underwriters a lot of money: it possibly saved one of the world's masterpieces from destruction. The incident happened when the Leonardo da Vinci cartoon was exhibited at Burlington House as part of the campaign to raise £800,000 to keep it in the country. 'One day the gallery got a letter from a crank,' says Gordon, 'saying he was going to damage it because he thought the money could be better spent. Because of the warning, we asked the gallery if they'd cover it with perspex just in case. They didn't like the idea but agreed. A few weeks later someone threw a bottle of ink at it. The claim was seventeen quid, instead of £800,000.'

As befits a man who relies on the confidence of some of Europe's leading policemen, Gordon's discretion is consummate. There are cases, he says, when a client wants to insure his wife's jewels, and his mistress's as well. 'Often the mistress's jewellery is better than his wife's, but we never put her name on the slip—they're just known as Client A and Client B. You can do something like this in Lloyd's, and no underwriter would ever divulge it.'

'If they're out in enclosed fields and not brought in at night, we'd want fifteen shillings per cent. And that,' said Mr Terry Hall cheerfully, 'would include theft or Mysterious Disappearance.'

In the mercantile world of Lloyd's the work of the livestock underwriter may seem to strike a pastoral note, but is by no means always peaceful. Nowadays when more animals than humans are carried around the world by sea and air, racehorses have to be insured against the harrowing possibility of their going berserk in aircraft. Even farmers have to insure against theft—'With meat prices what they are at the moment,' says Mr Hall, 'it's the easiest thing in the world for somebody to come along at night and fill a lorry with a thousand pounds' worth of beef.'

Mr Hall, a relaxed man with a red carnation who looks a bit like a farmer himself, has been writing livestock risks since 1949. A number of marine syndicates write some livestock, but Mr Hall is the specialist—among the policies he has pioneered are those which insure a cattle farmer against his herd getting brucellosis, and a poultry farmer against fowl pest. Meanwhile the really big premium income is from racehorse owners, particularly in the United States. The most expensive cover on his books at the moment, Mr Hall said, was for over $6 million on a three-year-old called Secretariat, the favourite for the Kentucky Derby.

I asked him what had been his most outlandish risk, and he said he supposed it had been when a whisky firm had offered a million-pound prize to anyone who could actually produce the Loch Ness monster. 'After they'd offered the prize, they suddenly got cold feet. It occurred to them that somebody might actually claim it. We took two-and-a-half thousand premium off them, and I warranted that the monster had to be caught by fair angling, which means by rod and line. It also had to be twenty feet long, and approved by the Natural History Museum. The last bit we put in as a joke—we said it had to be produced live, and handed over to the underwriters as salvage.'

Apart from such cheerful excursions into fantasy, the livestock underwriter needs to be an expert in his subject. Mr Hall reads the *Veterinary Record* every week, and consults some of the top vets in the country when he needs specialist advice. The day I saw him, he had just sent one out to Hungary to assess a loss. Over the importation of a sensitive breed like Charollais cattle, he said, he worked very closely with the Ministry of Agriculture.

I sat next to Mr Hall while a stream of brokers came up to the box: what with policies on prize bulldogs, pumas and guppy fish, it was a bit like an insurance man's Noah's Ark. The first broker said he had now got the answer to a query they had had the previous day, about a kind of bird called a trumpeter.

'That's right. We thought it was a sort of swan, didn't we?'

'Apparently it's more like a small crane.'

Mr Hall scribbled a note on a bit of paper, initialled the slip, and looked at a sheet of telex. It was from a client who wanted to renew the insurance on a lot of cattle and horses somewhere in Andalusia, but apparently thought the rate should be cut.

'He won't learn, will he.' Mr Hall studied the telex sadly. 'I like José, but there's nothing doing.'

Another broker moved to the top of the queue—he wanted to know how much it would cost to include the berserk clause on a racehorse travelling by air.

'Point one two five per cent. Half-a-crown.'

The broker asked if you spelt berserk with a 'z', and Mr Hall said no, with an 's'. 'It's an old Norse word. From when the Vikings used to fight each other. They went all bleary-eyed and frothing.'

'Sounds like a Lloyd's broker,' said the broker, and moved off.

The next man had a claim on some ostriches that had been taken by air from South Africa to the United States. It seemed two had broken their legs in transit, and had to be destroyed. Mr Hall said on this one he honestly thought they had a case against the shipper.

'It says here that the shipper is not responsible for death due to natural causes. That suggests that he is responsible if it's not a natural cause.'

They both went into a long discussion about what a natural cause was, then decided they'd go away and think about it. Afterwards I asked Mr Hall what would happen, and he said that in livestock insurance a dead animal was really nine-tenths of a claim. 'In a case like this, we'll honour the claim. Then we'll try to get something back from the shipper later.'

Recently it was estimated that the premium income to the London market from all livestock insurance is in the region of £5 million, of which Lloyd's takes a good deal more than half.

Given such an impressively large share of the market, I asked Mr Hall, what were the hazards in his business?

Much the worst in his experience, said Mr Hall, had been the outbreak of foot-and-mouth disease in the winter of 1967. The most serious epidemic for two hundred years, it had been the livestock underwriter's equivalent of Hurricane Betsy. 'The premiums were coming in at the rate of £10,000 a day. We didn't even count them. We used to pile them on the desk, feet high, then measure them with a ruler.' Despite the massive amount of premiums pouring in, the syndicate had made a heavy loss, and had to ask their names for money. Lloyd's underwriters as a whole had lost £300,000 before the market had – in his view, wrongly – baled out.

'What we should have done,' says Mr Hall, 'was to go on writing the business, because sooner or later the tide would have turned. In those days, foot-and-mouth insurance was comparatively new to me, but I've learned more now. If it ever happened again, I'd put my head down, and go on writing. Sooner or later, you write yourself out of trouble.'

One person out of five in Britain insures his car with one of the thirty syndicates in Lloyd's motor market. Though premiums are obviously smaller, profits are not necessarily less. Unlike other markets at Lloyd's motor insurers accept the whole liability and get the whole premium. 'My basic risk is the man in the street,' says Mr Sandy Lane of the Red Star syndicate, 'and we've got a devil of a lot of them.' Apart from men-in-the-street, Mr Lane's policies include one for a fleet of 10,000 small vans for a company in the Midlands, and another for 9,000 disabled drivers' cars for the Ministry of Social Security.

The motor market differs in several respects from others in Lloyd's. Because there is no standard motor policy, syndicates are allowed to be named—the assumption being that people like to identify their policy with something that sounds like a company and not merely somebody's surname.

A more important difference is that a broker does not have to come to the Room to place his risk. The Red Star syndicate has branch offices at Croydon and Birmingham, where underwriters can issue policies and deal, either directly or by post, with accredited brokers anywhere in the country. Nor do motor policies have to go through Lloyd's Policy Signing Office—with thousands of small policies, explained Mr Lane, it would not be worth it. Though motor policies do not bear Lloyd's seal, they have its full authority. 'There's just as much unlimited liability on a motor claim,' says Mr Lane, 'as there is for a Jumbo jet.'

Wasn't motor insurance, I asked, a bit cut-and-dried compared with most of the risks Lloyd's writes? Mr Lane looked a bit hurt and said he didn't think so. The window of his office in the Minories overlooked a site where there were lorries and an excavator going up a sharpish incline, laying the foundations for a new office block. 'I've been watching that excavator going up the slope there. For a motor insurance man, it's not a very reassuring sight.' Apart from excavators, he said, the motor insurer's daily round included such hazards as bulldozers, people with drunk convictions, company chairmen who wanted cover for their seventeen-year-old sons to drive a Maserati.

Another of his current problems was the big container trucks—now that so many of them were going abroad, he said, there were difficulties with foreign regulations. On the Continent a lorry could be liable for property damage to an unlimited amount, which meant that if a gasoline tanker blew up, the insurer could be in for a million. 'The forty-ton lorry drivers are first-class, but you have to remember that when they get across the Channel they're basically sitting on the wrong side of the truck.' Apart from the container trucks, he had just written £200,000 each on five mobile cranes being built at Sunderland to go to Eastern Europe. 'You don't just sit down and write that sort of cover by looking it up in a book.'

Would the average motorist get a better deal from Lloyd's

than from a company insurer? Mr Lane said he didn't think it was so much a question of a better deal as that with Lloyd's you had more contact. 'A client's introduced by a broker, who from then on looks after his interests. If you're insured directly with a company and something goes wrong, you've got no buffer. Here, you've got the broker who'll call a round-table conference if necessary, between the three of you. Moreover, it doesn't cost you any more to have a broker. His commission comes out of my premium.'

Motor syndicates tend to be busy. I sat on the Red Star box with Mr David Trotter, the deputy underwriter. Most of the time there was a queue of brokers.

One of them put a letter in front of Mr Trotter and said that this one was a bit involved: the client was eighty-five, and his policy was due for renewal. The problem was that because of his age he had to have an annual medical, and he was going to be abroad during the month the renewal came up. Could the underwriters give him an extra month's cover and renew the policy on condition he had the medical when he got back?

Mr Trotter shook his head sympathetically, and said he was sorry. 'If he was seventy-five, yes, but not eighty-five. I'm afraid he'll have to have his medical before we renew it.' The next renewal was from somebody who had previously had a claim for £210 on their Austin Mini: the owner's nineteen-year-old son had been driving.

'He's written a letter saying his son's not driving the car now,' said the broker hopefully. 'He wants to know if you'll delete the load.'

Mr Trotter said he was quite happy to delete it as long as the nineteen-year-old wasn't driving. I asked what was meant exactly by the load. Mr Trotter explained that this was about the only part of Lloyd's market where you did look up the rates in a book, but even then they were subject to what was called a load, or extra premium.

'There's a basic rate which is assessed on the value and power of the car and where the owner lives. Then we put on various loads according to the age of the driver, his claims record, and so on.' The lowest rate would be for a Mini when the owner lived in the country, and the most expensive for a sports car in London. I asked what would be absolutely the top rate of all and he said he supposed it would be for a Lamborghini whose nineteen-year-old owner lived in Hampstead. 'You'd ask for a premium around £1,000 with a large excess. Personally,' said Mr Trotter with a shudder, 'I'd try and get out of writing it.'

The Red Star syndicate's rating of districts is based on built-up areas; although there may be more risk of a head-on collision in a country lane, there is more possibility of Third Party liability in towns. 'You get people stepping off pavements, especially children,' said Mr Trotter. He showed me a book which the syndicate keeps, showing the whole country divided into different rates—London, for example, is graded seven, while Brecknockshire and Cornwall are graded one. If you live in Lancashire south of the River Ribble you pay rather more than if you live north of Morecambe Bay.

I asked what sort of drivers need special rating. Much the most difficult, Mr Trotter told me, were those for young drivers. 'Our view is that we're not happy about insuring anyone under twenty-one unless we also do their father. If we insure the family, then we feel it's our duty to give an indication of what rate we'd ask.' If somebody who has been insured with the syndicate for a long time gets a drunk-in-charge conviction, they will put him back on the road, though probably at a higher premium. This will vary according to the seriousness of the conviction. Mr Trotter said that if somebody had been breathalysed after having a few glasses of wine at dinner, he'd probably give them a £50 excess. 'On the other hand if they were absolutely paralytic, say 240 milligrammes over the limit, I'd make it for Third Party Bodily Injury only—which is the minimum basic cover demanded by the law.'

In a lot of ways the motor market is like a shop window for Lloyd's. A broker, said Mr Trotter, might be trying to place some very big risk for a company he hadn't dealt with before. 'The managing director might say, "I don't know anything about you, but my car's coming up for insurance. If you can get me good terms on that, we'll talk about the other business later." Car insurance can be a foot in the door for a broker—and if we can, we help him.'

What did he see as the special advantage of insuring at Lloyd's? Mr Trotter made the point about personal contact that Mr Lane had made earlier, and added that at Lloyd's it was often possible to get a cheaper rate. 'There are thirty-two motor boxes in the Room, and all of them have different rates. If you go to a broker, he can try as many as he needs to.'

The other thing, he said, was the integrity of Lloyd's—it wouldn't go bust, as some car insurance firms had been known to. 'The liability's unlimited just the same. Whether you're insuring a petro-chemical plant or the family car.'

Meanwhile the queue of brokers was getting longer. Mr Trotter took the next slip that was offered.

'Let's get this straight. He's got himself a company car. And the wife's sold her old banger?'

Coming after the guppy fish and Ming vases, it all seemed positively homely.

9
'Touching the Adventures and Perils . . .'

> Touching the Adventures and Perils which we the Assurers are contented to bear and do take upon us in this Voyage, they are, of the Seas, Men-of-War, Fire, Enemies, Pirates, Rovers, Thieves, Jettisons, Letters of Mart and Countermart, Surprisals, Takings at Sea, Arrests, Restraints and Detainments of all Kings, Princes and People, of what Nation, Condition or Quality soever, Barratry of the Master and Mariners and of all other Perils, Losses and Misfortunes . . .

SUCH, in the words of Lloyd's Marine Insurance Policy of 1779, were the Adventures and Perils—the possible disasters which a ship-owner could claim for.

Today, nearly two hundred years later, the range of possibilities is somewhat greater. It may not include Barratry of the Master, Letters of Mart or Pirates. On the other hand the twentieth century can all too easily produce its own equivalents, from hijacking to war risks and earthquakes to pollution.

In a single week of 1950 Lloyd's paid $28 million for American storm losses. Fifteen years later, when Hurricane Betsy tore into the Atlantic coast, their share was $100 million. Such huge sums may be the exception, but even in an ordinary year well over £600 million worth of claims are made on Lloyd's underwriters.

The story of how they are assessed, worked out and paid, is the story of Lloyd's Claims Office.

'Mind you don't shift that manhole. There's still gas in her holds.'

From somewhere down the Rhine waterway came the wailing, scraping sound of a dredger; in the great Verolme shipyard a sparkle of blue acetylene flared and died against the winter sky. Mr Harry Thurston, the Ship Surveyor at Rotterdam, adjusted his tin hat, then led the way into the burnt-out afterhouse. It was a bit like going into a stalactite cave, eerie, dark, with bits of twisted metal hanging from the ceiling.

'That was the electric control for pumping the oil.' Mr Thurston flicked on his torch and we peered into a blackened room that led from the deckhouse. You could just see the outline of what had been the control panel, swollen and shapeless like a slab of stone.

We came out from the afterhouse to the deck—everywhere there was a reddish soil-like substance where the bitumen surface had melted. The afterhouse windows had caved in so it had the look of a ruined castle. Halfway along the deck a couple of men were hauling up cans of sludge on a sort of pulley.

Of all the Perils and Adventures listed in the Lloyd's policy of 1779 there is still one that is a terrifying word to any seaman, and that is fire. It was fire which had struck this ship, the *Trilantic*. She had been bound for Leixoes in Portugal from the Persian Gulf with a load of crude oil six months before when fire had broken out in her engine room. One man had been killed, the duty engineer, who had stayed in the engine room to try to turn off the oil valves. The rest of the crew had been picked up by a Russian tanker, and the still-smouldering *Trilantic* towed to Gibraltar. From there she had been brought to Rotterdam for her oil to be discharged. Now the long and complicated task of surveying her was beginning.

As we picked our way gingerly down the twisted companionways, Mr Thurston explained that he was not strictly speaking employed by Lloyd's—the Salvage Association, which he represents in Rotterdam, is an organization looking after the interests of all London underwriters. In this case the ship had been insured at Lloyd's. If she was eventually written off as a total loss, the claim would be in the region of $10 million.

'Do you think she will be a total loss?' Looking down the great length of deck it seemed likely. Of all inanimate objects few things are sadder than a ship that has been swept by fire.

'It's a question of what the owner decides.' Mr Thurston explained that there had already been long discussions with the owner—even the actual decision to bring the *Trilantic* to Rotterdam had been worked out in consultation between him and the Salvage Association. The reason for this was that the *Trilantic* was not a conventional tanker but what was called an OBO.

'It isn't a kind of musical instrument.' Mr Thurston comes from Hartlepool; after 21 years abroad he still has a hint of the bent vowels of the north-east. 'It stands for an Oil Bulk Ore carrier. The point is that her holds are specially constructed.' Because of this, he explained, there had been a considerable problem about discharging her cargo of 68,000 tons of crude oil. If it hadn't been done in exactly the right way, she could have keeled over while being emptied in the dry dock. Eventually it had been decided that only the port of Rotterdam had the necessary facilities.

Now that the oil had been safely discharged, the next thing would be to see how badly she was damaged—the owners' fear, Mr Thurston said, was that her whole stern quarter might have been pushed out of alignment. 'In that case he might have to rebuild the whole stern and afterhouse, which would cost more than she's insured for.' A lot of tests had been carried out, he said, in dry-dock—now she was afloat again and there would be more tests. One way and another it looked like being a fairly complicated claim, but so were most of the claims that came his way as a Ship Surveyor. In his office at Schiedam he had four surveyors working under him, and they dealt with everything from colliding coasters to recovering cargoes from ships that had been stranded.

If the Salvage Association was instructed by Lloyd's, I asked, wasn't any survey bound to be biased in favour of the underwriter and against the owner? Mr Thurston stressed very strongly that it wasn't—the Latin motto of the Association, he said, meant 'Seek the Truth', and they meant it. In the twenty years he had been with the Salvage Association he had always seen his job as to make sure that all claims were settled fairly and reasonably, and he couldn't remember one that wasn't.

All his life, Mr Thurston said, he had had a twin passion for ships and football. Before working for the Salvage Assocation he had been a ship's engineer with the Blue Funnel Line, then with smaller tramp steamers operating from his home town. 'I gravitated back to my original level,' he said, with a grin, 'West Hartlepool.' Since joining the Salvage Association he had worked in Cardiff, Antwerp, Hamburg and Rotterdam, where for the last five years he had run a football club called the Pirates made up of a mixture of Dutch, English and Belgians. All the same, the team he really supported was from just about the only place he had never worked in—Manchester United.

Meanwhile, he suggested that if I'd like to put on my tin hat again we might go down and have a look at the engine room. There wasn't much to see, but a few technicians were down there working on the engine alignment. We went down a couple more companionways, then along a stretch of metal deck which had been bent and buckled so there was water lying in deep puddles. Then we were in the dark again. When we emerged it was into a huge area like a great cave.

'This was the engine room.' Mr Thurston looked round. There were a few naked bulbs but the light only made it seem more garish. Everywhere there was blackened metal and blistered bulkheads. In the centre were the seven cylinders of what had been the ship's main engine.

'The water came right up to the height of those cylinders.' Mr Thurston shone his torch towards them, and I peered down. They must have been forty feet up.

We edged slowly down a ripped-up platform, then down a

ladder. With bits of metal hanging over us at head height, I could see the point of the tin hats.

'Like Dante's *Inferno* the day after.' Mr Thurston shone his torch into a small, blackened control room—it was here, he said, that the duty engineer had died in the fire. 'This is where it started. Like the pillar of flame in the Bible. It must have just gone through the deckhouse in minutes.'

He flicked off the torch, and we made our way slowly back along the blackened companionways. After the grimness of the burnt-out engine room, even the cold wind on deck was a relief. In the distance the coasters slid past the entrance of the Rhine waterway—the deceptive calmness, it occurred to me, of a world of ships.

'Touching the Perils which are of the Seas, Men-of-War, Fire . . .'

After two hundred years, they seemed as real as ever.

The *Trilantic* might be called an extreme example. It is not every shipping casualty where salvage experts are called to supervise so delicate an operation as the discharge of 68,000 tons of oil from a ship which could have keeled over. Even then, highly sophisticated techniques were going to be needed to assess possible damage to the *Trilantic*'s hull. But if the *Trilantic* is an extreme case, so is every other. Because of the enormous variety of risks written at Lloyd's, and because of all the things that can go wrong, hardly any two claims are alike. What the story of the *Trilantic* shows above all is the range of skills needed in assessing them.

Meanwhile what is the actual procedure when a claim is made? It will come first to the Claims Office, opposite the main building of Lloyd's; it occupies two floors of a building called Excess House, which might sound a bit orgiastic for insurance men. If it is a marine casualty, it will come through the office of Mr W. F. Pearson, the Marine Adjustor. More than 80 per cent of all claims are settled in full, and on most of the rest there will be an agreed compromise. 'We're here to settle claims,' says Mr Pearson firmly, 'not reject them.'

The first news of a casualty comes from the broker who will have had a telex from the owner. Most often he takes one copy to Mr Pearson's office and another to the Salvage Association. The Association, acting as we saw on behalf of underwriters, will instruct a surveyor. In a big port like Rotterdam or Piraeus the surveyor will be someone on their regular staff. In a smaller port the Association will contact a local surveyor through Lloyd's agents.

'What the Salvage Association surveyor really does,' explained Mr Pearson, 'is to oversee and report on anything to do with a ship from the moment she becomes a casualty. Supposing she's gone aground—she'll have to be refloated. After that she may be towed or go under her own power to the nearest port. In that case the owner may need to take tenders and the surveyor will tell us the cost. When the repairs are done, it's his job to see that they're done properly.' Subject to the policy, he said, all this would ultimately be paid for by the underwriters.

While I was talking to Mr Pearson various brokers were arriving with claims or queries. Apart from these, another member of his staff was going through an enormous folder containing about 150 foolscap pages.

This, Mr Pearson said, was called an Adjustment of General Average—it was one of the more recondite bits of insurance procedure, and practically impossible to explain to a layman. If I really wanted him to, he'd have a try: to understand General Average you had to think of a voyage as a whole, or, as it was called in the eighteenth century, an Adventure. In that Adventure a lot of things were involved—the ship's hull and what might be several different kinds of cargo. General Average was really a parcelling-out of everyone's interests. Supposing a ship caught fire and part of her cargo was high explosives, the master might decide to dump it for the safety of the rest of the ship. That part of the cargo would be totally lost, whereas the ship itself and the rest of the cargo might be only slightly damaged. The Average Adjustor's job would be to work out the value of the dumped cargo in relation to the rest. From there he would apportion the liability among the underwriters concerned. If I hadn't understood it, Mr Pearson said, he didn't think I need worry—there were only about twenty-five people in the City who did.

Meanwhile more brokers had been arriving. One had brought a surveyor's report on a Greek ship stranded in the Persian Gulf. Mr Pearson said this was one he had dealt with before and he was pretty sure she would be a constructive total loss.

I said that sounded a bit of a contradiction in terms. He laughed and explained that there were two sorts of total losses. 'An actual total loss is where the ship has sunk—there's no doubt about it. A constructive total loss means she's so badly damaged that the cost of repairing and refloating her would be more than the insured value.'

I asked what would happen to the stranded ship in the Persian Gulf, and he said the chances were that someone would buy her and break her up for scrap metal. If that did happen, the underwriter might get some of the salvage. Once he had received the settlement of his claim, the owner was bound to disclose any subsequent proceeds.

He broke off to talk to an underwriter who had come in to discuss a claim. It was something to do with excess-of-loss on a dam in California. Evidently there had been a good deal of discussion about it before, and the underwriter shook his head gloomily. 'I was so convinced we'd never have to pay this claim.'

'If you will write this sort of business in California,' said Mr Pearson, and they both laughed rather wryly, but even the underwriter, I noticed, seemed a little in awe of the expertise of the Claims Office.

When the underwriter had gone Mr Pearson said he had to make a phone call to the Salvage Association. They had phoned earlier to know whether he wanted them to get statements from the crew of a ship which had just sunk off Cuba.

'What's the idea of getting crew's statements?'

Mr Pearson looked rather cautious and said he'd rather I didn't mention the name of the ship, but she was sailing under the Liberian flag and had sunk in what had apparently been a flat calm. 'When that happens we tend to be very careful. There are a few owners, not many, who might throw away a ship.'

'Throw it away?'

'Scuttle it,' said Mr Pearson mildly. 'If so, one way you can find out what's happened is to take statements from the crew. The trouble is that once you do that, it looks as if you're starting an investigation.'

By this time he had got the Salvage Association on the line. He listened while they went over the details again, then nodded. 'Frankly I'm a bit inclined to wait and see on this one. Can we get a bit more information on the weather?'

It seemed that the Salvage Association could. They had already been in touch with Lloyd's agents on the spot.

'Tell the local agent,' said Mr Pearson cautiously, 'he might listen out for a bit of galley talk. Otherwise I don't think at this stage there's any reason for going further.'

How often, I asked, did they get a fairly clear case of someone deliberately sinking a ship? Out of four hundred total losses a year, Mr Pearson said, there might be perhaps two or three thrown away, and even those might not reach the stage of litigation. Sometimes in a doubtful case underwriters would rather pay the claim than make trouble. 'You'd do as much damage by fighting an unsuccessful case as you would settling a doubtful loss.'

What made someone decide to throw away a ship, and what sort of people were they? Mr Pearson looked rather tolerant and thought the market would be hesitant to condemn people. A ship-owner might be in all kinds of difficulties that could make him want to throw away a worn-out ship, and there were a dozen different ways of doing so. Usually he would rely on the sort of faults produced by wear-and-tear. At other times, Mr Pearson said, he'd pay a crew. In the Caribbean not too long ago there were some well-known characters who could be got together as crew by a not very scrupulous owner. Their names appeared a few times on casualty reports. 'After a while, we got to know them.'

'Are they still around?'

'Oh yes,' Mr Pearson nodded sedately. 'They're still around. If we see their names on a crew-list we're on our guard.'

I said goodbye to Mr Pearson and walked out into Lime Street, wondering who it was who had said that insurance was a dull business. Whoever it was, he hadn't met the mild-mannered men of Excess House.

What happens if a claim has to be negotiated? With the kind of risks Lloyd's deals in, settlement is not always quite as straightforward as if the ordinary person makes a claim, for instance, on his car.

If there does need to be discussion on a claim, it will come on the desk of an energetic Scot named Dick Rutherford. As head of Lloyd's Underwriters Claims Office he is ultimately responsible for all marine claims and often others—Mr Rutherford says he was born under the sign of Pisces, which ought to make him sea-going. In fact he spends a lot of his time in aircraft, travelling between London and the United States, and anywhere else you care to name. 'With the vast volume of claims that go through the market,' he explained, 'not all fall strictly within the contract. If the facts don't clearly establish a loss, then it's our job to arrive at a fair compromise.'

I asked Mr Rutherford to give me an example of the sort of case where this might be necessary, and he pointed out that nowadays the market increasingly has to deal with the sort of claim for which there are few legal precedents. 'When you have a case of marine law,' he said, 'it will have been established and contested in countless court cases. When you're dealing with a hijacked aircraft or oil pollution, the ground is not so well worn.'

One case that is still being discussed in the US Courts is that of the Boeing 747 blown up in 1970 at Cairo Airport by Arab hijackers. The problem here, Mr Rutherford explained, was that the Boeing was insured under two different policies—first an All-Risks policy, which despite its name does not include war risks, and also under a separate War Risk policy. Though in each case the owners, Pan Am, had insured for $24,000,000, the placing of the risks varied. The greater part of the All-Risks insurance was in the American market. In the case of the War Risk policy, more than two-thirds was at Lloyd's. The risk had been led by one of the market's most respected syndicates, headed by a now-retired underwriter named Roy Merrett.

'The ambiguity that arose,' says Rutherford, 'was that the plane was seized by the PFLP which claims to be an organization fighting on behalf of exiled Palestinians. So was the liability on the War Risk or the All-Risks policy? If the PFLP was deemed to be criminal, then the liability would fall on the All-Risks policy, which included criminal action. But if a court decided they were a political organization, then it would count as a War Risk.'

Meanwhile it was clear that Pan Am was entitled to a claim under *one* of the two policies. Roy Merrett had come up with the suggestion that each set of underwriters should contribute half. The Lloyd's men agreed, but Merrett had not been able to persuade the American underwriters, who feared that any immediate payment would prejudice their final position.

Eventually Roy Merrett and the other War Risk underwriters had made an interim payment of $7 million, pending the American court's decision. 'Their view,' says Rutherford, 'was that the airline was entitled to prompt recompense under one policy or the other. It seemed unfair that they should lose out because of a dispute between two sets of underwriters.'

Another example of the kind of risk that can produce endless legal complexity is that of oil pollution. When oil from the *Torrey Canyon* flooded British and French beaches in 1969, Lloyd's underwriters were not only liable for the loss of the ship—they were asked by the British and French governments for compensation in the region of £6 million. This was not only to cover such things as the use of the RAF and the clearing of oil from the beaches. Compensation, the governments said, had to be made to hotel-keepers, fishermen and people who hired boats out. In the end Lloyd's and the other underwriters concerned settled for £3 million. 'How do you assess loss of revenue to an ice-cream man,' asks Rutherford, 'when his loss might be due to the fact that it was a bad summer?'

Perhaps the oddest claims story is that of the £11 million which Lloyd's underwriters paid on fifteen ships which are still afloat. The story begins in January 1967, at the time of the Six-Day War between Israel and Egypt, when the ships became trapped in the Suez Canal.

From the beginning of the battle it had been part of Egyptian strategy to block the Canal. To this end they had sunk two ships in the narrows roughly at the centre of the Canal near Ismailia. During the fighting, five other ships had been sunk—two 8,000-ton passenger ships at the north end of the Canal near Port Said, and a small tanker, a tug and a dredger at the south end.

At the time the fighting began, fifteen neutral ships had been passing through the Canal. To complicate things still further, one of them, the US ship *Observer*, had gone aground in Lake Timsa. Her grounding was nothing to do with the fighting, though in normal circumstances she would have been soon refloated. The fourteen other ships, including four British, were all trapped in the bulge of the Canal, which is known, from the salts in it, as the Great Bitter Lake.

This was the position of the ships at the end of the Six-Day War, and so it remained right through till the following summer.

The United Nations had agreed that the Canal should be cleared and the vessels released as soon as possible, but that was all. An Egyptian attempt to investigate the possibility of clearing the northern exit had been stopped by Israeli shellfire.

That, by the end of 1967, was the position; meanwhile, what could Lloyd's, as the main insurers, do? At this stage the hull underwriters were not so much affected as those who had insured the cargoes. Their worry was that the ships contained huge amounts of fruit and other perishables. If these were not released soon, there could be a heavy loss on the cargoes.

Meanwhile a Lloyd's broker knew – and at Lloyd's there is always someone who knows somebody – an Egyptian named Dr El Hefnaoui who was legal adviser to the Suez Canal Authority. In the spring of 1968 Dr El Hefnaoui had talks in London with leading underwriters and Rutherford. As a result, a three-man party left for Suez in April. They found the Egyptians both helpful and hospitable, but with Israeli guns trained across the Canal, there could, they decided, be no hope of getting the ships out except by agreement with both sides.

Before they left, the Lloyd's party visited the ships, which were still manned by skeleton crews, who mostly amused themselves, Rutherford recalls, by holding regattas. One of the sadder touches of the story had come a few weeks before on the anniversary of the Six-Day War. All of the fourteen ships in the Great Bitter Lake had formed themselves up and gone round the lake in procession, sirens moaning, to draw attention to their plight. On board the ships, the Lloyd's party sampled the apples and pears from the cargoes. 'We brought some back, but they were all bad,' Rutherford said. 'I remember we tried them at the weekly meeting of the Marine Claims Adjustors.'

If any agreement was to be made, Lloyd's next step was to contact the Israelis. Already in the Cairo meetings they had had the help of a Labour MP, Tam Dalyell, who now arranged a meeting with the Foreign Secretary, the Rt Hon. Michael Stewart. The meeting took place at the Foreign Office on

April 8. The Foreign Secretary listened sympathetically and told the Lloyd's delegation that there were already moves about the ships going on at the United Nations in New York. Meanwhile he thought it might help if Lloyd's were to approach the Israelis.

The Lloyd's party arrived in Tel Aviv at the end of April to find the Israeli government helpful and sympathetic as the Egyptians had been, but adamant on one point. This was that any exit of the ships must be from the south end of the Canal, whereas the Egyptians had insisted on the north.

'Partly,' says Rutherford, 'the Israelis genuinely feared that if the north end was cleared, it could open up a supply line from Russia to Egypt. At the same time, we all had a feeling that both sides were going to do the opposite of what the other wanted.'

Thus the Lloyd's delegation were faced with stalemate. Either they could tactfully try to persuade the Egyptians to allow the southern channel to be cleared, or similarly try to persuade the Israelis to clear the northern one. Either way they ran the risk of offending one side by seeming to let themselves be used to press the case of the other.

By the middle of the summer there was no sign of a shift in the political situation. In June, Lloyd's announced that they would now settle the claims on the cargoes, amounting to five million pounds.

Meanwhile, various further attempts went on to persuade the Egyptians to allow an exit by the south. Around the beginning of 1969 there seemed a real chance they might do so. A Dutch salvage firm was brought in to advise on the technical problems. Plans and estimates of cost began to be drawn up. Then, on 12 March 1969, fighting again broke out across the Canal.

For the Lloyd's delegation, it was the beginning of the end. The next few months dragged out in anticlimax. In August 1969, Lloyd's announced that the underwriters concerned had unanimously agreed to settle. But now came what was in one way the most interesting question—how far were Lloyd's liable to pay any claims at all? 'Strictly speaking,' says Rutherford, 'the ships were insured against total loss, and in terms of the policy they had to be lost by way of a peril. The only peril they'd suffered was that they'd been bottled up. On the other hand if people pay premiums they're entitled to get something back. In the end we settled on all the ships at around seventy per cent. All the same it cost Lloyd's close on eleven million.'

Do the crews of the fifteen ships still sometimes start their rusting engines, form themselves into line and circle the aptly named Great Bitter Lake? If they ever are released they will be almost valueless. The cargoes, on the other hand, could yield a profit. Though the fruit has long since rotted, several of the ships carried valuable metal cargoes, the price of which has soared since 1967.

Profit or not, the important thing about the odd story of the Suez ships, Mr Rutherford says, is that Lloyd's tried. 'It was very important for all the things Lloyd's stands for that we should have done our best, then acted magnanimously when we failed.'

Meanwhile there is one other episode which cannot be left out of any account of Lloyd's—not only for its own sake, but because it exemplifies the combination of good taste and gritty professionalism which is the essence of Lloyd's style.

The story of the Indonesian ships – or to be strictly accurate the prologue to it – begins in October 1957. In that month Roy Merrett, a leading war-risk underwriter, was approached by a broker friend named John Wallrock. Wallrock was trying to place some reinsurance for the newly formed national insurance company of Indonesia, known by its initials as UMUM. The broker was having a certain amount of difficulty in placing the business—could Roy Merrett help?

No Lloyd's underwriter likes to think of good premiums going to waste. At the same time, Roy Merrett, who happened to be a particularly shrewd observer of the world political scene, remembered something he had noted in his diary a year before —that Indonesia was a quarter of the world from which, sooner or later, trouble could be expected. Nevertheless he told the broker he would do what he could for UMUM. Next day, John Wallrock came to his office and introduced Dr Tjoa Sie Hwie, the head of the Indonesian company.

What exactly were the difficulties facing UMUM? Essentially they were implicit in Indonesia's new-found independence. A former colony of the Dutch, it had become a sovereign state under the Hague Agreement of 1949. Though many Dutch business firms had stayed on in the capital, Jakarta, there had lately been rising tension over the territory of Western New Guinea, which had remained under Dutch control by the terms of the Hague Agreement. In 1956, fifteen Afro-Asian states had urged that the question of its independence should go to the United Nations. The previous April, a newly elected Indonesian government, reflecting the increasing nationalistic mood, had set up a Western New Guinea Liberation Committee.

How did all this particularly affect UMUM? Like all national insurance companies in emergent countries, it urgently needed to spread its load of risks by reinsurance. The trouble was that most of the Indonesian links were with Dutch insurers, and by this time relations with Holland were clearly worsening. Moreover, the Dutch underwriters resented the loss of business to UMUM, and refused to help the new company by reinsuring. Dr Tjoa had gone to several other continental insurers, found them unwilling to offend the Dutch, then come on to London. Several broking firms had tried to place the business for him at Lloyd's. But like the continental underwriters, the market did not want to spoil its good relations with the Dutch. Almost as a last throw the broker had approached Roy Merrett.

From the first moment the two men established a rapport. Roy Merrett, now a benign and sprightly seventy-year-old, recalls their first meeting. 'For the first hour we talked a lot of the time about theosophy. I found Dr Tjoa immensely able and intelligent—a man of great integrity.'

By the end of the hour's talk, Merrett had decided to lead the risk. 'I put my terms to him and he didn't argue. He said if I thought they were fair it was good enough for him.'

Thus in October 1957 the reinsurance had been placed. Roy Merrett had led the risk and been supported by the market. On October 16 he noted in his diary that Dr Tjoa and his assistant had come to his office to thank him. If he ever had occasion to visit Indonesia, said Dr Tjoa, Roy Merrett would be most welcome.

In Jakarta itself events were now moving fast. In the middle of November a huge political rally urged the government to take strong action against the Dutch over the Western New Guinea question, and on the last day of the month an attempt was made to assassinate President Soekarno. It was unsuccessful, but triggered off a new wave of nationalism. In the first week of December Dutch-owned banks, hotels and offices were seized by a rioting mob, and the red flag flown from them.

Among the main targets – and it was this which concerned Lloyd's – was the office of the shipping firm KPM. Short for Koninklijke Paketvaart Maatschappij, this was the company operating the main steamer service between the islands that make up the Indonesian archipelago. Most of their fleet was insured in the London market, with the largest share at Lloyd's. On December 7, *Lloyd's List* carried a brief news item saying that all Dutch ships had been ordered to remain in Indonesian harbours. Within a week half the KPM fleet – around forty ships – had been arrested and were under military control.

At first the Lloyd's market seems scarcely to have reacted. Forty-odd ships lying bottled up in harbour did not, after all, suggest anything as ominous as a total loss. Roy Merrett himself recalls that his own first hint of anxiety came on December 6, when he noticed that there were rather a lot of brokers around the Room trying to place reinsurance on the KPM fleet. He got the feeling, he noted in his diary, that the Dutch underwriters were getting worried and wanted to unload some of their liability on to the London market.

Why, when the ships were after all in no danger of sinking, should there have been any anxiety at all? The point was that the KPM policies carried one rather unusual clause. Known as the 'four months clause', it had arisen when Dutch owners had become anxious about the possibility of their ships being seized in the Baltic. In the 1950s, the cold war was still on. Dutch brokers have the reputation of being more adroit than most, and it had been a Dutch broker who had noticed that ships trading to countries like Latvia and Finland ran a certain risk of being held by the communists. He had persuaded underwriters to add a clause protecting them from such an arrest for the addition of a tiny extra premium. From then on it had been written into most Dutch policies, including those of the KPM, that if a ship was held for longer than four months, she would count as a total loss.

Now, a week after their seizure, there was no sign of the ships being released. It began to look as if the four months clause might be invoked in a set of circumstances which no one had imagined, and a very long way from the Iron Curtain. The full horror of the situation began to dawn on the Room. In their worst moments, no underwriter had ever imagined the total loss of forty ships of the same fleet. With the complexities of reinsurance nobody quite knew what the possible claim might be, but it was clearly in the range of £11 million; one syndicate alone stood to lose half a million. The marine market began to view things with the nearest Lloyd's ever gets to consternation.

A sub-committee of marine underwriters was formed. On December 10 it was agreed that an approach should be made to the Foreign Office. 'Basically,' says Roy Merrett, 'the only chance of getting the ships released hung on one point. If we could persuade the Indonesians that by keeping the ships they were hitting at Lloyd's and not the Dutch, then there might be a chance. What was essential was that Lloyd's should be able to put its case to the people who mattered in the Indonesian government.'

One of the other underwriters who had a line on the ships was Paul Dixey, now Chairman of Lloyd's. At Dunmow in Essex, he had once been to a tea party with his friend and neighbour, Kingsley Martin. Among the guests had been Dr Subandrio, then Indonesian Ambassador to London. Dixey had talked to him, and later shown him round Lloyd's.

Now, five years later, Dr Subandrio was the Indonesian Foreign Minister. The link seemed tenuous, but potentially useful if, as Merrett and Dixey had already discussed, Lloyd's sent a mission to Jakarta. Nothing else seemed likely to help. *The Times*, in a leader called 'The New Piracy', accused the Indonesian government of playing what it called 'a cat-and-mouse game with the Dutch-owned shipping service that supplies half the islands'. 'Along the KPM wharves,' wrote the paper's Jakarta correspondent on December 19, 'the ships lie idle in a long silent row . . . while dark-skinned workers sit on their hands beside sheds which are also idle and silent.'

In London, Paul Dixey got a dusty answer from the Foreign Office to the suggestion that a party of underwriters might go out. 'They could hardly have been more damping,' he recalls. 'They said they couldn't possibly be involved in a quarrel between the Indonesians and the Dutch. Beyond that, they were quite certain we hadn't got a chance.'

Meanwhile – and it is at this point that the whole exercise begins to be a particularly immaculate example of Lloyd's combination of self-interest with charm – Roy Merrett had also approached his broker friend who had first introduced him to Dr Tjoa, and reminded him of Dr Tjoa's invitation to stay with him if he ever had occasion to visit Indonesia.

Now, in the last week of December, it began to look as if Roy Merrett might indeed have occasion to visit Indonesia.

What would help above all, he decided, was a specific invitation. John Wallrock cabled Dr Tjoa on Merrett's behalf, and on January 27 the reply came back. Would Merrett and some of his friends care to visit Jakarta for the Chinese New Year?

On February 11 the delegation left London. Led by Roy Merrett, it consisted of two other underwriters, Paul Dixey and Harold Hopwood; Hugh Mitchell of Lloyd's Claims Office and A. W. Green of the Commercial Union, which also had a line on the ships. Paul Dixey had taken the trouble to arm himself with letters of introduction from Dorothy Woodman who, besides being Kingsley Martin's wife, was the *New Statesman*'s expert on south-east Asia. 'I remember asking her,' recalls Dixey, 'whether she thought it proper for a leading left-wing journalist to help a group of capitalists. She roared with laughter.'

No sooner had the delegation arrived at Singapore than they struck trouble. The news from Indonesia was that a new coup seemed likely, stemming from the policies of a revolutionary group based on Central Sumatra. The local diplomatic advice was for the delegation to stay put in Singapore and see what happened. Wisely, as things turned out, they ignored it and decided to push on.

By the time they reached Jakarta the threat of the coup had somewhat faded, but the delegation had problems of their own. Roy Merrett, who had planned the whole operation, had been taken ill in Karachi. By now he was in a boiling fever. A Chinese doctor pronounced him suffering from dysentery, and said it would be unthinkable for him to stay as the guest of Dr Tjoa, whose wife was pregnant. Madame Tjoa's reaction was typical of the whole rapport that existed between Lloyd's and the Indonesians—she not only refused to let him leave the house, but nursed him herself till he was over the fever.

Clearly the delegation's presence in Jakarta was officially known, but there was no sign of government reaction. Soon after their arrival Dixey rang up the Foreign Minister's wife and reminded her that they had met in Essex. 'She said how splendid, and that we must come round,' says Dixey. 'After that, we heard nothing.'

For the next few weeks the delegation sat around, answering any questions they were asked about the policy on the ships, and, as one of them put it, 'not muddying the channel'. One day Paul Dixey went to see one of his contacts, a woman who had been secretary to the Cabinet. 'We chatted about everything except the KPM ships,' he recalls. 'At the end of the interview, she asked if I'd been to the port where the ships were —it occurred to her that I might have a special interest in them. She said it with a terrific twinkle.' Looking back, Roy Merrett thinks that one of the main things working to the delegation's advantage was the general Asian assumption that Britain had displayed considerable intelligence and goodwill over the granting of independence to India. 'I think they contrasted this with the way the Dutch had behaved in Indonesia,' he says. 'It was one of the things that most helped us.'

Above all there was no hint of a threat, no suggestion that Lloyd's were in a position to damage Indonesia's interests in the future. When the subject of the seized ships did come up, the delegation quietly stated their point that by keeping them, the Indonesians would be harming not the Dutch, but Lloyd's. The last thing the Dutch wanted was the return of forty decaying and damaged ships which were certainly going to be unable to sail the routes for which most of them had been built. 'When you think of it,' says Merrett, 'there was a tremendous element of ironic comedy in our situation. Most British businessmen would have been rushing round trying to contact other British businessmen who knew the ropes out there. We relied on what most people in the City would have called the wrong people.'

Each night in the bungalow, Merrett and Dr Tjoa talked over the progress, or lack of it, made each day. Between such talks the delegation spent a lot of time at the UMUM office, helping the company produce a standard policy for hulls.

Coming from a group of men whose basic object was to save £11 million, it was a good example of casting your bread upon the waters.

Meanwhile the weeks slipped by, with the April deadline approaching and the four months clause ticking away like a time-bomb. On March 10 Merrett noted in his diary that they didn't feel optimistic. Dixey also began to lose heart: the Indonesians, he felt, were simply stringing them along. 'All they had to do was wait till the four months was up, then Lloyd's would have to pay the loss. After that the ships would become the property of the underwriters, and the best they could hope was that the Indonesians would buy them back cheaply.'

On March 12, Dr Tjoa told Roy Merrett at their evening conference that the government had come up with a specific request. Urged on by some of their more militant supporters, they wanted confirmation in writing that Lloyd's would be liable for a total loss after the four-month period. It was arranged that Dixey should return to London, show the original policies to the Indonesian Ambassador, then return. After nearly five weeks the delegation seemed almost back to the beginning.

The evening before he was due to go back to London, Dixey rang Madame Subandrio again. 'We still had one ace in our pack, and I decided to play it.' He told her he was going back to London and was sorry to do so without seeing her husband.

'But he *does* want to see you.' She would ring her husband at his office now, Madame Subandrio said, then ring Dixey back at UMUM.

Dixey hung around the UMUM office for more than an hour. It was just on midday, and the whole of Jakarta was about to close down. Meanwhile he wanted to get some presents to take home, and flowers for people who had been helpful in Jakarta. In the absence of a phone call from the Foreign Minister's wife, he decided to go and get them before the shops shut. He left the office, went down a couple of staircases, then remembered he hadn't got the address of someone he wanted to send flowers to. He went back upstairs to the empty office, found the address, and was just about to leave again when the phone rang. It was Madame Subandrio. Would Dixey call round that evening before he left and bring his friends?

Back at Dr Tjoa's house, the delegation held a council of war —even now, they were convinced there was little chance of anything happening. In the evening Merrett, Dixey and Harold Hopwood set off in drenching rain. In the car on the way Roy Merrett gave the others a piece of advice which summed up the delegation's approach. 'Remember,' he said, 'we'll play it our way. We're not going to mention those ships.'

When they arrived at the Foreign Minister's villa, Dr Subandrio gave them a glass of orange juice, enquired after mutual friends and then asked why Dixey was going back to London. Dixey said he was going to produce some insurance policies for the Ambassador there, and Dr Subandrio looked surprised.

'Then he said the words I'll never forget,' says Dixey. 'He said, "But you know we're going to give you back those ships." I don't know how low you can get and then go whizzing up to the heights. But that's what we did.'

In the event it took another month before the matter of the forty ships was settled. Dixey returned to London and showed the Ambassador the policies. On March 20 Roy Merrett, who stayed on with the others, in Jakarta, recorded in his diary: 'Dr Tjoa came in with great news.' It was that the government had officially decreed the release of the ships. On March 22, *Lloyd's List* reported, in characteristically deadpan style, that Indonesia had 'formally handed back thirty-four impounded ships of N.V. Koninklijke Paketvaart Maatschappij'.

A week later the delegation went down to the Tandjong Docks and drank a farewell glass of orange juice with one of the Dutch captains. 'I said how delighted he must be to be going,' recalls Merrett, 'and for the first time in all our jubilation there was a note of sadness. The captain said he'd been in Indonesia a very long time and he minded going. One of the Indonesians who was there said he was sorry to see him go as well. In the midst of all the trouble there'd been, there were some very real relationships.'

But by now the saga of the Indonesian ships was almost over. On March 31 Merrett cruised round the harbour in a launch watching the last of the vessels being got ready for sailing. Three days later he sent a telex to Lloyd's confirming that they had all left, except one which had mechanical trouble at Surabaya, and three others which were still in outlying ports.

The whole episode had some agreeable by-products. When the delegation got back to Lloyd's, they were given a presentation by the Room. The following year Lloyd's was able to make a return gesture to the Indonesian government over a difficult insurance on tobacco products, and relations continue to flourish. Roy Merrett became the godfather of Madame Tjoa's baby. He still visits the family regularly and the picture of his godson occupies a prominent position on his mantelpiece, next to the clock given him by his grateful colleagues in the Room.

In the end the Indonesian affair could be called the definitive exercise in Lloyd's style. It is also probably the only major commercial deal in history which depended on a talk about theosophy, a tea party in an Essex village and a bunch of flowers.

10
The Market Tomorrow

TILL now we have looked at Lloyd's from the point of view of an outsider looking in. How do the market's prospects look to those on the inside? Essentially, if Lloyd's is to continue in its 300-year-old tradition it must remain commercially viable. The function of any market is to make, and to be seen to make, profits.

Looking back over the modern story of Lloyd's there are two periods of great change. The first of these we have already seen—the period around the 1900s when non-marine insurance began to be written in the Room, and when the first links with America began to be forged.

The second period of change produced less obvious results, but it was almost as far-reaching. Even after the Second World War, a Lloyd's underwriter could still arrive at his box around ten o'clock in the morning and go home at four, having earned substantial profits in agreeable surroundings without too much effort. 'There's no doubt,' said one underwriter, 'that for a long time a lot of people were feather-bedded. What weeded out the layabouts was the losses of the mid-1960s.'

Why did Lloyd's make such losses in what are still referred to in the Room with a faint shudder as the Lean Years? The first and most obvious reason was a long run of major disasters in the United States. The worst of these, as we have seen, was Hurricane Betsy, but there were also fires, floods and race riots. Both marine and non-marine markets were badly hit, especially in the field of reinsurance. To allow for claims to come in, Lloyd's does its accounting on a three-year basis. The full horror of the situation did not dawn until 1968, when Lloyd's global returns showed a loss of £38 million on its 1965 dealings.

How – even given such an across-the-board disaster as Hurricane Betsy – could Lloyd's lose quite so much? Most underwriters now admit that the big profits of the early 'sixties had led to careless underwriting. There was no doubt that they failed to recognize the acceleration of inflation. Thus when they came to pay claims, the cost was far higher than when they fixed the rate of premium.

By the late 1960s, world insurers had learned the lesson of Hurricane Betsy. The rates went up, and Lloyd's was able to charge a more realistic premium. But meanwhile underwriters faced a new problem. Frightened off by the 1968 results, not enough new names were coming forward. Unless he has sufficient names to back him, the underwriter is limited in the amount of premium income he can write. In 1968 a Working Party was set up, headed by Lord Cromer. Its basic finding was that Lloyd's problem was capacity. More names, in other words, must be encouraged to join the syndicates.

In response to the need for capacity, Lloyd's decided to admit first foreign, then women members: though it rejected a proposal from the working party to allow companies to become members of syndicates, provided their share in any one was not more than 10 per cent. A limited liability company, the Committee felt, could hardly be subject to the unlimited liability which Lloyd's insists upon.

Since the Cromer Report Lloyd's premium income has continued to increase. The 1968 account, published in 1971, showed a profit of £35 million on a premium income of £668 million. In 1972 this increased to a profit of £52 million on a premium income of £693 million. The increase in capacity has kept up with the 10 per cent growth rate set by Cromer.* In many other

* Ironically, such expansion has brought its own problems. One aviation underwriter told me his syndicate had attracted a lot of names when aviation rates were high. Now, because of increased safety records, they were much lower, and his problem was to spread the profits.

ways, and particularly under the recent chairmanship of Sir Henry Mance, Lloyd's has modernized its approach. Apart from the introduction of foreign and women members, the last five years has seen a great increase in the use of new techniques such as the streamlining of its Accounting System, and indeed in the whole role of the Corporation.

Meanwhile what about the problems the market faces in the future? Unlike a conventional insurance company, Lloyd's cannot offset its losses in a bad year by income from investment. Nor, since the names are paid their profits on a yearly basis, can it subsidize bad years with the gains from good years. One answer to both problems could be the 'catastrophe fund' which has often been suggested—though to date no progress has been made with it because of the intricate tax problems involved.

If such a fund were created, it could greatly help Lloyd's to meet what is increasingly the problem of modern insurance, the sheer size of risk. Nowadays a container ship may carry a cargo that a few years ago would have been spread among several vessels. In the same way a jumbo jet can carry the equivalent of the number of people carried by five aircraft a few years ago. 'The loss of one jumbo with no survivors,' says Mr David Gilmour, a leading aviation underwriter, 'would in one accident exceed all passenger fatalities from jets in commercial operations for the whole of 1971.'

Another problem facing the whole insurance market is inflation. Because of it the underwriter is often facing both ways —he has to keep his rates down to compete, yet must be always looking over his shoulder to see what inflation may do to his claims. 'Although inflation will not add to what I might pay on a total loss,' said one marine underwriter, 'it can mean huge increases on a claim for partial damage. Suppose I insure a ship, and a year later she's stuck in Barcelona with a bent propeller. She'll have to be dry-docked, then perhaps have to have a new propeller brought from Hamburg. The cost of manufacturing the propeller, of transport and of dry-dock facilities will have all gone up. The underwriter has got to allow for all this, yet keep his rates competitive.'

Although such problems are real, one is conscious of a total confidence that Lloyd's can overcome them, as it has done others in the past. 'The same characteristics that made us famous in the days of sailing vessels are there today,' says Paul Dixey. 'There is the collective wisdom, the willingness to pioneer new types of cover. Today there are still classes of insurance for which Lloyd's is the only market.'

Added to the long tradition there is a new sense of professionalism in the Room. I asked Peter Foden-Pattinson, one of the youngest and liveliest members of Lloyd's Committee, what he thought was the greatest asset for the future. 'If you ask anybody in the world,' he said, 'they'll tell you that in this building there's more insurance expertise collected than in any other single place. It's like a university of insurance. Above all Lloyd's lives by its quick reactions—what I'd call its general coming-in-out-of-the-rain sense.'

No great institution can exist without change. How is Lloyd's, which has so often adapted to change in the past, likely to do so in the future? Many Lloyd's men feel that the time is past when an underwriter should only be seen sitting at his box. They would like underwriters to travel more widely, meeting the people whose risks they write. Lloyd's has, for instance, established a Common Market Secretariat. Mr H. H. T. Hudson, Deputy Chairman of Lloyd's, suggested that with more brokers opening up offices in Europe, there was no reason why underwriters should not accept business on the spot. 'It seems logical, now the brokers are able to extend themselves into the EEC countries, that underwriters should do so too.'

Other people see the future as producing a greater stress on loss prevention. As the Intelligence Department has helped with safety at sea, so Lloyd's Loss Prevention Office has begun to influence the market in ways of crime prevention. In fire insurance there is an increasing stress on safety. 'In the future,' said one underwriter, 'I believe we shall be looking not at how much a claim is going to cost, but at how we can advise a client to help prevent it happening. In this way we should not only be doing ourselves good. We should be serving the public interest.'

If the physical structure of the Room were changed, Lloyd's would hardly be Lloyd's, but there are many who feel that the problem of queues of brokers must be overcome in some way. One leading jewellery underwriter told me he had a ghastly feeling that Lloyd's might eventually see several syndicates clubbing together, with a principal underwriter for each main class of business. 'The broker would know that on a straightforward risk he could get a million pounds' worth of cover at one box. At the moment if a broker wants a couple of million he's got to see about thirty people, which means queueing at all their boxes. In this way he could do it in a quarter of an hour.'

A lot of people feel there should be some means of storing information, which could be made available to underwriters at their boxes. At the moment the tendency is for underwriters to keep their own statistics which they show to no one else. 'What it amounts to,' said one, 'is that you get a lot of people knowing most of the things they need to know, but nobody knowing all of it. If the information was pooled, a computer could feed it all into a central bank. Underwriters would still be able to keep their own statistics and compare them with the pooled ones.'

Because of the sheer physical shortage of space, it seems conceivable that if such a method was introduced, an underwriter at his box might one day tap out a question and get the answer on a TV screen. Such a device might clash a little with the Lutine Bell and the red-robed waiters, but would not be out of keeping with the Room's traditional ability to adapt. What would be unthinkable to Lloyd's men would be any radical change in the physical structure of the Room, and especially of the boxes. With his overheads at a fraction of what those of a conventional company would be, the underwriter's box is not merely a ritual symbol. It is Lloyd's secret weapon in the world's competitive markets.

I went into the Room for a last look round: the great Room whose occupants over the years have coloured the world of commerce with originality and a touch of romance, and added the dimension of style to the business of making money. It was after half past four. Except for a small queue at a leading underwriter's box, the stream of brokers was thinning.

On the Casualty Boards the yellow, pink and blue notices announced the day's consignment of destruction—floods, fires, earthquakes, riots. An underwriter and a broker were looking at them. After a moment somebody came up and showed a note to the underwriter, who nodded, then turned to the broker.

'We had an arrival,' he said, and the broker laughed. They might have been talking about anything from the safe landing of a cargo to the opening of a trade fair, but the old maritime phrase seemed to span Lloyd's history.

Whatever it was that had arrived, it was time for my departure. I said goodbye to the waiter on the door, and went out into the winter sunlight.

Glossary

A Layman's Guide to Insurance Terms

Assured Anyone whose life or property is protected by insurance. Although the words insurance and assurance are interchangeable the latter is used more often in connection with life business.

Audit Lloyd's Audit was introduced in 1908 with the object of ensuring the individual solvency of the underwriting accounts of all Members of Lloyd's.

Broker An insurance broker places insurance on behalf of a client. As the agent of the insured his job is to obtain the best terms he can. His only obligations to underwriters, by whom he is paid on a commission basis, are those of good faith and responsibility for premiums.

Captive Used in the same sense as a captive audience. Some large organizations paying considerable sums in premiums have found it worthwhile to set up a company specifically to handle their insurance. Examples are to be found within ICI and among a number of the big oil companies.

Consequential Loss A fire which destroys a factory could, in addition to the cost of rebuilding, mean a loss of profits to the owner. A normal fire policy might cover plant and machinery, but consequential insurance would also compensate the owner for any loss of revenue.

Correspondent A local broker, usually in the United States, who can place business in the market through a Lloyd's broker.

Deductible The specified proportion of any claim which is to be borne by the assured: for example, most motor insurance policies specify that the insured will pay the first £10 of any claim.

Excess of Loss A form of reinsurance (*q.v.*) by which an underwriter can protect himself against loss above a given amount. This type of business is often done in layers involving more than one reinsurer. For example, an underwriter having written a risk for £60,000 may wish to limit his liability to, say, £20,000. He can do this by getting another underwriter to cover him for £20,000 for any claim in excess of £20,000. Then he might get a third underwriter to cover the remaining £20,000. Thus a claim for £50,000 would cost the first underwriter £20,000, the second £20,000 and the third £10,000. Excess of loss reinsurance was devised by C. E. Heath following heavy claims arising from the San Francisco earthquake.

Hull For insurance purposes this is the ship itself excluding the engines. Underwriters also speak of the 'hull' of an aircraft.

Infidelity Not, as one underwriter explained, what they mean by it in Knightsbridge, but a breach of trust on the part of an employee.

Line The amount of an underwriter's liability. They write and initial the proportion of the risk they are willing to accept on one line of a slip.

Lloyd's Agent Agents of the Corporation of Lloyd's. Their primary duty is to keep Lloyd's informed of shipping movements, casualties and other matters of interest to insurers and the commercial community generally. They also survey damaged cargo and some agents have authority to settle cargo claims.

Lloyd's Underwriting Agency A Lloyd's underwriter will accept risks on behalf of many Names, but his staff, accounts and investment of premium income will all need management. This is provided by underwriting agency companies. The underwriting agency does not accept risks but fulfils a purely administrative function.

Loading An increase in premium to cover an increase in risk. A larger premium, for instance, may be required for young or inexperienced motorists.

Name A term usually applied to an Underwriting Member of Lloyd's who need not necessarily be actively engaged in the market, but participates as a 'name' on a syndicate.

Policy Legal evidence of the agreement to insure which may be produced by the insured in court to press a claim against the insurer.

Premium The sum of money paid by the assured to the insurer in return for compensation in the event of loss from an insured peril.

Premium Income Income derived by underwriters from their premiums. The current annual premium income of Lloyd's is now well in excess of £700 million.

Producer Another word for correspondent (*q.v.*).

Reinsurance When an underwriter has written a line on a slip he becomes liable for any loss which may occur on that insurance. He may seek to lay off some of his liability by insuring it in turn with other underwriters who then become his reinsurers.

Slip A slip of paper used by brokers for placing an insurance. It contains brief details of the risk on which underwriters write their lines. Until recently the slip was a somewhat undisciplined document but a standardized version is now rapidly gaining acceptance.

Syndicate For practical reasons members of Lloyd's group themselves into syndicates. Some syndicates consist of hundreds of Members, some of only a handful. Some are specialists in one class of risk; most write a broad spread of business.

Underwriter One who accepts liability for insurance. The name is derived from the time-honoured practice by which underwriters write their names one under another on the slip. Usually implies a Member of Lloyd's, but can be a paid employee of either a Lloyd's syndicate or an insurance company who works as an underwriter.

War Risks Technically these include capture, seizure, arrest, restraint or detainment of princes or peoples, men of war, engines of war, mines, torpedoes or any hostile act. War risks on land is one of the very few insurances which may not be underwritten at Lloyd's or by any commercial body.

Wet Risks A phrase spanning the somewhat grey area between marine and non-marine. A non-marine risk having the smell of the sea about it such as dams, piers, wharves and bridges.

Index